GROUND MOTIONS AND SOIL LIQUEFACTION DURING EARTHQUAKES

Monograph Series

Engineering Monographs on Earthquake Criteria, Structural Design, and Strong Motion Records

Coordinating Editor, Mihran S. Agbabian

Monographs Available

Reading and Interpreting Strong Motion Accelerograms, by Donald E. Hudson

Dynamics of Structures—A Primer, by Anil K. Chopra

Earthquake Spectra and Design, by Nathan M. Newmark and William J. Hall

Earthquake Design Criteria, by George W. Housner and Paul C. Jennings

Ground Motions and Soil Liquefaction during Earthquakes, by H. Bolton Seed and I.M. Idriss

GROUND MOTIONS AND SOIL

LIQUEFACTION DURING

EARTHQUAKES

by **H. Bolton Seed**
Department of Civil Engineering
University of California, Berkeley

and **I. M. Idriss**
Woodward-Clyde Consultants
Santa Ana, California

EARTHQUAKE ENGINEERING RESEARCH INSTITUTE

Published by

The Earthquake Engineering Research Institute, whose objectives are the advancement of the science and practice of earthquake engineering and the solution of national earthquake engineering problems.

This is volume five of a series titled: Engineering Monographs on Earthquake Criteria, Structural Design, and Strong Motion Records.

The publication of this monograph was supported by a grant from the *National Science Foundation*.

Library of Congress Catalog Card Number 82-84224
ISBN 0-943198-24-0

This monograph may be obtained from:
Earthquake Engineering Research Institute
2620 Telegraph Avenue
Berkeley, California 94704

FOREWORD

The occurrence of earthquakes poses a hazard to urban and rural areas that can lead to disaster unless appropriate engineering countermeasures are employed. To provide an adequate degree of safety at an affordable cost requires a high level of expertise in earthquake engineering and this in turn requires an extensive knowledge of the properties of strong earthquakes, the influences of soil conditions on ground motions, and the dynamics of structures that are moved by ground shaking. To achieve this it is necessary for relevant information to be published in an appropriate form.

This monograph by H. B. Seed and I. M. Idriss on the effects of soil conditions on ground motions and liquefaction during earthquakes is the fifth in a series of monographs on different aspects of earthquake engineering. The monographs are by experts especially qualified to prepare expositions of the subjects. Each monograph covers a single topic, with more thorough treatment than would be given to it in a textbook on earthquake engineering. The monograph series grew out of the seminars on earthquake engineering that were organized by the Earthquake Engineering Research Institute and presented to some 2,000 engineers. The seminars were given in 8 localities which had requested them: Los Angeles, San Francisco, Chicago, Washington, D.C., Seattle, St. Louis, Mayaguez, P.R., and Houston. The seminars were aimed at acquainting engineers, building officials and members of government agencies with the basics of earthquake engineering. In the course of these seminars it became apparent that a more detailed written presentation would be of value to those wishing to study earthquake engineering, and this led to the monograph project. The present monograph discusses the role of local soil conditions in determining the characteristics of earthquake ground motions to be used in engineering design, and the liquefaction or cyclic mobility potential of soil deposits due to earthquake shaking.

5

The EERI monograph project, and also the seminar series, were supported by the National Science Foundation. EERI member M. S. Agbabian served as Coordinator of the seminar series and is Coordinating Editor of the monograph project. Technical editor for the series is J. W. Athey; graphics by G. Lillegraven and E. Harding. Each monograph is reviewed by the members of the Monograph Committee: M.S. Agbabian, G.V. Berg, R.W. Clough, H.J. Degenkolb, G.W. Housner, and C.W. Pinkham, with the objective of maintaining a high standard of presentation.

Monograph Committee
GEORGE HOUSNER, *Chairman*

Pasadena, California
December, 1982

PREFACE

The influence of soils on the behavior of structures during earthquakes received very little attention from geotechnical engineers until the early 1960's. However, a series of catastrophic failures, involving landslides at Anchorage, Valdez and Seward in the 1964 Alaska earthquake, extensive liquefaction in Niigata, Japan during the earthquake near there in 1964, and the remarkable relationship between the intensity of structural damage and local soil conditions in Caracas, Venezuela during the 1967 Caracas earthquake stimulated enormous interest in the general field of earthquake soil dynamics. Fostered by the public concern for the safety of nuclear power plants, the recent interest in the safety of dams and most especially by the establishment of the National Science Foundation program on Earthquake Hazards Mitigation, research and design studies have grown dramatically until they now represent a significant portion of the work of many geotechnical engineering companies and research organizations. As interest and activity have grown, there has developed a need for a simple and straightforward presentation of design practices and considerations in earthquake geotechnical engineering. This monograph was prepared to fill this need. It is not intended to provide an exhaustive discussion of the subjects covered but rather to point out the essential elements in a manner that can be readily understood by engineers with no particular familiarity with the field. We hope it will in this respect be helpful to the civil engineering profession.

H. BOLTON SEED

I. M. IDRISS

Tilting and settlement of a building in Niigata, Japan, as a result of soil liquefaction in the 1964 Niigata Earthquake.

CONTENTS

Figure 1. Partially submerged island near Valdivia, Chile (1960).

Figure 2. Differential settlement between bridge abutment and backfill, Niigata (1964)

12

Ground Motions and Soil Liquefaction During Earthquakes

H. Bolton Seed *and* **I. M. Idriss**

INTRODUCTION

The damage resulting from earthquakes may be influenced in a number of ways by the characteristics of the soils in the affected area. Where the damage is related to a gross instability of the soil, resulting in permanent movements of the ground surface, association of the damage with the local soil conditions is readily apparent. Thus, for example, deposits of loose granular soils may be compacted by the ground vibrations induced by the earthquake, resulting in large settlements and differential settlements of the ground surface. Typical examples of damage due to this cause are shown in Figs. 1 and 2. Figure 1 shows an island near Valdivia, Chile, which was partially submerged as a result of the combined effects of tectonic land movements and ground settlement due to compaction in the Chilean earthquake of 1960. Figure 2 shows differential settlement of the backfill of a bridge in the Niigata, Japan, earthquake of 1964.

In cases where the soil consists of loose granular materials, the tendency to compact may result in the development of excess hydrostatic pore water pressures of sufficient magnitude to cause liquefaction of the soil, resulting in settlements and tilting of structures as illustrated in Fig. 3. Liquefaction of loose saturated sand deposits resulted in major damage to thousands of buildings in Niigata in 1964 (Ohsaki, 1966).

The combination of dynamic stresses and induced pore water pressures in deposits of soft clay and sands may result in major landslides such as that which developed in the Turnagain Heights area of Anchorage, Alaska, during the earthquake of March 27, 1964 (Seed and Wilson, 1967). An aerial view of the slide

13

Figure 3. Tilting of apartment buildings, Niigata (1964)

Figure 4. Turnagain Heights landslide, Anchorage, Alaska (1964).

14

area is shown in Fig. 4. The coastline in this area was marked by bluffs some 70 ft high sloping at about 1 on 1½ down to the bay. The slide induced by the earthquake extended almost 2 miles along the coast and extended inland an average distance of about 900 ft. The total area within the slide zone was thus about 130 acres. Within the slide area the original ground surface was completely devastated by displacements that broke up the ground into a complex system of ridges and depressions. In the depressed areas the ground dropped an average of 35 ft during the sliding. Houses in the area, some of which moved laterally as much as five or six hundred feet as the slide progressed, were completely destroyed. Major landslides of this type have been responsible for much damage and loss of life during earthquakes.

While the role of the soil conditions is readily apparent in cases of soil instability such as those described above, a less obvious effect of soil conditions on building damage is the influence they exert on the characteristics of earthquake ground motions and thereby on the structural damage that may develop even though the soils underlying a building remain stable during an earthquake.

It has long been recognized, for example, that the intensity of ground shaking during earthquakes and the associated damage to buildings are influenced by local geologic and soil conditions. MacMurdo (1824), in describing the effects of the earthquake near the Runn of Cutch, India, in 1819, noted that "buildings situated on rock were not by any means so much affected by the earthquake as those whose foundations did not reach to the bottom of the soil." Inferential evidence that the soil conditions underlying a site can have a substantial effect on the intensity of ground surface motions was also presented by Wood (1908) in his study of the distribution of damage and apparent intensity of shaking in the San Francisco Bay area during the earthquake of 1906. Since that time a number of investigators have presented similar results.

It has only been in the last 25 years, however, that strong motion instrumental records have been obtained at a number of locations in the same general area to show the major effects of variations in local soil conditions on the characteristics of strong

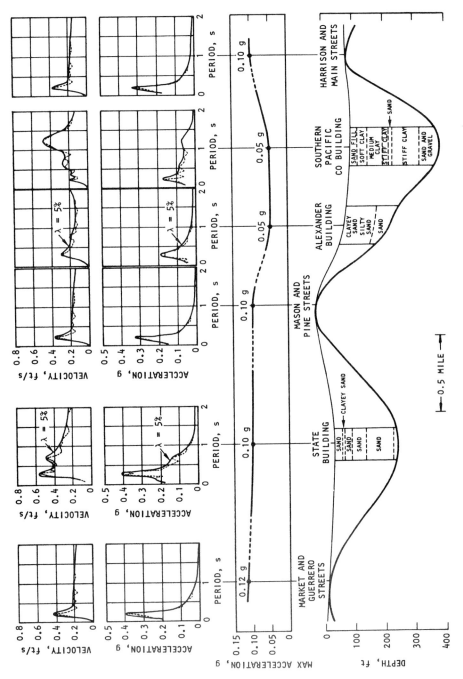

Figure 5. Soil conditions and characteristics of recorded ground motions, San Francisco earthquake, 1957.

16

ground surface motions. In the 1957 San Franciso earthquake (M ≈ 5.3), for example, recordings of ground motions were made at several locations within the city (Idriss and Seed, 1968). The variations in soil conditions along a 4-mile section through the city and corresponding variations in recorded ground shaking characteristics are shown in Fig. 5. It is readily apparent that significant variations occurred both in the peak accelerations developed and in the frequency characteristics, as illustrated by the response spectra for the recorded motions. Using the recorded motions as a basis for analysis, computations show that the maximum base shear for a typical 10-story building located

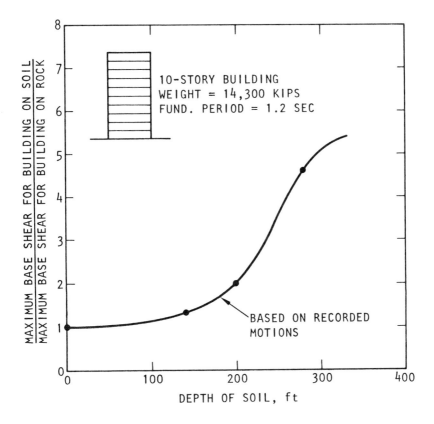

Figure 6. Influence of soil depth on maximum base shear for 10-story building in San Francisco earthquake of 1957.

17

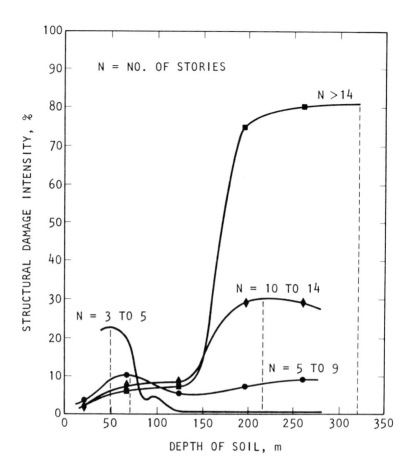

Figure 7. Relationship between structural damage intensity and soil depth in Caracas earthquake of 1967.

at each of the recording sites would vary by several hundred percent, from relatively low values for sites underlain by rock or shallow soils to much higher values at sites underlain by about 300 ft of clay and sand, as shown in Fig. 6. Clearly it is desirable to be able to anticipate variations of this magnitude at the design stage.

Probably the most detailed investigation of the relationship between building damage due to ground shaking and soil conditions was that made for Caracas following the Caracas earthquake of 1967. Although the magnitude of the earthquake was only about 6.4 and its epicenter was located about 35 miles from

Caracas, the shaking caused the collapse of four 10- to 12-story apartment buildings with the loss of over 200 lives. Many other structures suffered structural and architectural damage. A detailed study of the relationship between structural damage to buildings and the depths of the underlying soils led to the results shown in Fig. 7 (Seed and Alonso, 1974). For 3- to 5-story buildings, damage was many times greater where soil depths ranged from 30 to 50 meters than for soil depths over 100 meters. For 5- to 9-story buildings, the structural damage intensity was slightly higher for soil depths of 50 to 70 meters than for other depths of soil, but for buildings over 10 stories high, the structural damage intensity was several hundred percent higher where soil depths exceeded 160 meters than for soil depths below 140 meters. It would appear that the depth and characteristics of the underlying soil deposits had a significant effect on the characteristics of ground motions and the resulting building damage, although building characteristics are also very much involved in determining the damage patterns.

The magnitude of the influence of local soil conditions on the characteristics of earthquake ground motions and thereby on building damage merits their careful consideration in seismic design. Because this monograph cannot review all aspects of soil behavior during earthquakes, it will concentrate on the two topics of most general interest: (1) the influence of soil conditions on the characteristics of earthquake ground motions, and (2) methods of evaluating the liquefaction potential of soil deposits. The following chapters present a review of what the authors consider to be the current state-of-the-art information on these two subjects.

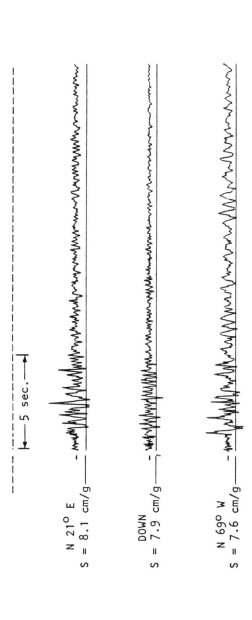

5 sec.

N 21° E
S = 8.1 cm/g

DOWN
S = 7.9 cm/g

N 69° W
S = 7.6 cm/g

NATIONAL OCEAN SURVEY NOAA
SEISMOLOGICAL FIELD SURVEY
CASTAIC, OLD RIDGE ROUTE
AR 240 S/N 124
EARTHQUAKE OF 9 FEB 1971   0600 PST

Figure 8. Typical accelerograph record.

20

Influence of Soil Conditions on Earthquake Ground Motions

Characteristics of Earthquake
Ground Motions

Information on the characteristics of earthquake ground motions is obtained from accelerograph records of past earthquakes. A typical accelerograph record of a ground motion, after digitization and replotting, is shown in Fig. 8. Typically such a record shows the acceleration time history of the ground in two horizontal directions (at right angles to each other) and the time history of vertical accelerations.

Each component of horizontal motion can readily be integrated with respect to time, with appropriate care to minimize sources of error, to obtain first the time history of ground velocity at the recording station and then the time history of displacements. Such motions, computed from a given time history of acceleration, are shown in Fig. 9.

From records, developed and processed as shown in Figs. 8 and 9, it is readily possible to read off some of the main characteristics of the ground motions, such as

1. Maximum ground acceleration
2. Maximum ground velocity
3. Maximum ground displacement
4. Duration of significant ground shaking.

These are all important characteristics of any ground motion but they alone do not describe the intensity of the shaking effects of the motion, which depend also on the frequency characteristics of the motion. For example, a very high acceleration may appear to be potentially hazardous, but if it is developed for only a very short period of time it will cause little damage to many types of structures. A good example of this is provided by the ground motion recorded near Parkfield, California, in the earthquake of June 27, 1966. The maximum ground acceleration

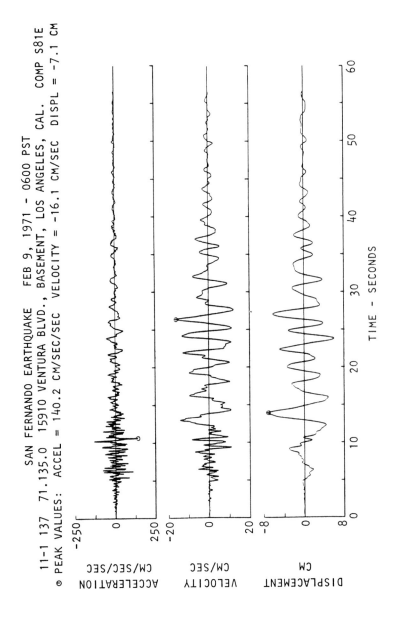

Figure 9. Typical corrected accelerogram and integrated velocity and displacement time histories.

22

reached a value of 0.5g but probably because of its high frequency and the short duration of ground shaking, no significant damage to buildings was reported (Cloud, 1967). On the other hand, a motion with a relatively small amplitude that continues with a reasonably uniform frequency for a number of seconds can build up damaging motions in certain types of structures. A good example of this effect is the damage to structures in Mexico City during the earthquake of July 28, 1957. The maximum ground acceleration in the central part of the city was estimated to be only about 0.05 to 0.1g (Merino y Coronado, 1957), but the frequency characteristics and duration were sufficient to cause the complete collapse of multistory structures (Rosenblueth, 1960).

The combined influence of the amplitude of ground accelerations, their frequency components and, to some extent, the duration of the ground shaking on different structures is conveniently represented by means of a response spectrum (e.g., Housner, 1952; Hudson, 1956 and 1979); that is, a plot showing the maximum response induced by the ground motion in single-degree-of-freedom oscillators of different fundamental periods, but having the same degree of internal damping. For example, the ground accelerations recorded in the El Centro earthquake of May 1940 are shown in the middle part of Fig. 10. If the three simple structures shown in the upper part of Fig. 10, having fundamental periods of 0.3, 0.5, and 1.0 sec and damping factors of 0.05 were subjected to this motion, the maximum accelerations developed in them would be 0.75g, 1.02g, and 0.48g, respectively. It is apparent that the maximum acceleration induced in simple structures of this type varies with the fundamental period of the structure. A graph showing the maximum accelerations induced in the entire range of such structures, with fundamental periods ranging from 0 to several seconds, is called an acceleration response spectrum. Such a graph for structures subjected to the ground motions recorded at El Centro is shown in the lower part of Fig. 10. The maximum accelerations for the structures shown in the upper part of Fig. 10, together with similar computations for structures with other fundamental periods, provide the means for plotting this response spectrum.

Clearly, similar computations could be made for structures

23

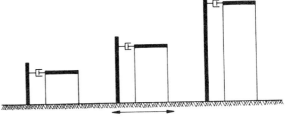

NATURAL PERIOD	T = 0.3 s	T = 0.5 s	T = 1.0 s
DAMPING FACTOR	$\lambda = 0.05$	$\lambda = 0.05$	$\lambda = 0.05$
MAXIMUM ACCN.	$\ddot{U}_{max} = 0.75$ g	$\ddot{U}_{max} = 1.02$ g	$\ddot{U}_{max} = 0.48$ g

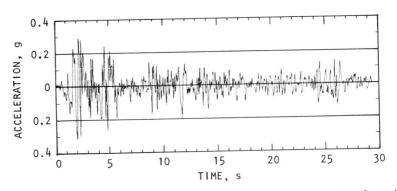

ACCELEROGRAM, EL CENTRO, CALIFORNIA EARTHQUAKE,   MAY 18, 1940
(N-S COMPONENT)

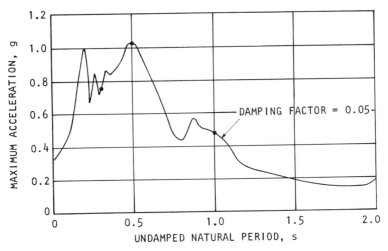

ACCELERATION RESPONSE SPECTRUM, EL CENTRO GROUND MOTIONS

Figure 10. Evaluation of acceleration response spectrum.

24

with a similar range of fundamental periods but having different degrees of internal damping. Thus it is customary to draw acceleration response spectra for a given ground motion for structures with several different degrees of internal damping, as shown in Fig. 11.

Similarly, the computations could be made to determine not the maximum accelerations but either the maximum induced velocities or the maximum displacements. A plot showing the relationship between the maximum velocity induced by a given base motion in single-degree-of-freedom structures having a given degree of damping and the fundamental periods of the structures is termed a velocity response spectrum; such a spectrum for the El Centro ground motions is shown in Fig. 12.

For any given ground motion, values of the spectral velocity S_v and the spectral acceleration S_a for a single-degree-of-freedom structure having a period T are related approximately by the equation

$$S_v \simeq \frac{T}{2\pi} \cdot S_a \qquad \text{for } 0 < T < 5 \text{ sec}$$

and it is therefore a simple matter to convert a velocity spectrum to an acceleration spectrum, or vice versa.

It can be seen from the above discussion that the time history of the ground motions at a site is characterized by the corre-

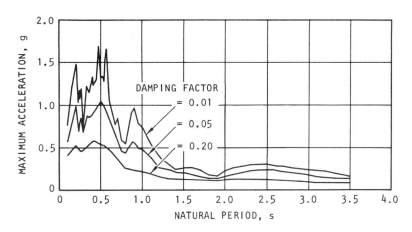

Figure 11. Acceleration response spectra for El Centro (1940) earthquake.

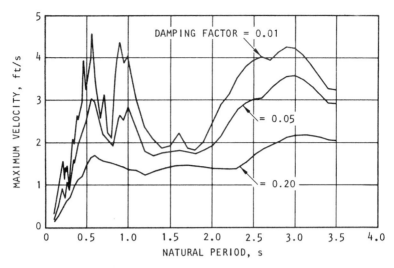

Figure 12. Velocity response spectra for El Centro (1940) earthquake.

sponding response spectrum. Thus, differences in the time histories of motions at different sites may be conveniently evaluated by a comparison of their response spectra. More importantly, however, a response spectrum provides a convenient means of evaluating the maximum lateral forces developed in structures subjected to a given base motion. If the structure behaves as a single-degree-of-freedom system, the maximum acceleration and thus the maximum inertia force may be determined directly from the acceleration response spectrum from a knowledge of the fundamental period of the structure. If the structure behaves as a multi-degree-of-freedom system, the maximum responses can be determined for a number of modes and the overall maximum evaluated by some appropriate combination of the different modal effects. Normally the first mode has the greatest influence on the maximum response, and thus the fundamental period, even for a multi-degree-of-freedom structure, has a dominant influence on the induced lateral forces.

For example, the maximum base shear, V_{max}, for a multi-story structure subjected to a given base motion can be estimated from the equation

$$V_{max} \simeq W \cdot \frac{S_a}{g}$$

where W is the weight of the structure, S_a is the spectral acceleration corresponding to the natural period of the structure,

26

and g is the acceleration of gravity. This relationship works reasonably well for a multistory structure even though the acceleration response spectrum is derived for single-degree-of-freedom systems.

It is apparent from the above discussion that the major earthquake parameter affecting the maximum base shear developed in a structure is the spectral acceleration, S_a. Thus the form of the response spectrum for a given ground motion is a major factor determining the lateral forces induced on engineering structures. Of particular importance in the acceleration response spectrum, for example, are the maximum ordinate and the fundamental period at which it occurs. This is readily illustrated by the data presented in Fig. 13. In the lower part of the figure are two ground motion records, one for a site in San Francisco in the San Francisco earthquake of 1957 and one recorded in Pasadena during the Kern County, California, earthquake of 1952. Both records show about the same maximum ground acceleration. The response spectra for these ground motions are shown in the upper part of the figure. It is readily apparent from the spectra that responses of structures to the two ground motions will be radically different. For example, the maximum acceleration induced by the San Francisco ground motion in a single-degree-of-freedom structure having a fundamental period of about 0.9 sec would be only 0.04g; the maximum acceleration induced by the Pasadena ground motion in the same structure is seen to be 0.2g, an increase of about 400 percent. From the point of view of determining the maximum accelerations and lateral forces developed on structures during earthquakes, the establishment of the correct form of the response spectrum is clearly of primary importance.

It can be noted in Fig. 13 that the ground motions compared were recorded at quite different epicentral distances. Studies by Housner (1959) have shown that the frequency characteristics of earthquake motions change with increasing distance from the epicenter or zone of energy release. As the waves travel through the ground the short period motions tend to be filtered out, with the result that the maximum ordinate of the response spectrum moves toward longer periods.

However, it should also be recognized that even for sites in

27

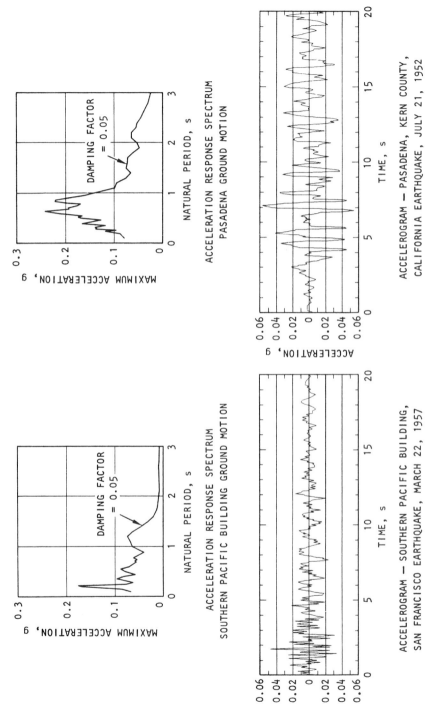

Figure 13. Accelerograms and acceleration response spectra for two ground motions with comparable maximum accelerations.

the same general area, the frequency characteristics of earth-quake ground motions, and therefore the form of the response spectrum, can be significantly influenced by the soil conditions underlying a site. This is an important effect that will be discussed in greater detail in the following pages. First, however, it is useful to examine the effects of soil conditions on some of the other characteristics of ground motions.

Factors Affecting Earthquake Ground Motions

The characteristics of earthquake ground motions at any site are influenced by a number of factors including:

1. Magnitude of the earthquake
2. Distance of the site from the source of energy release
3. Geologic characteristics of the rocks along the wave transmission path from source to site
4. Source mechanism of the earthquake
5. Wave interference effects related to the direction and speed of fault rupturing
6. Local soil conditions at the site.

The influence of some of these factors is better understood than others and, in fact, the detailed influences of some factors such as the source mechanism and the transmission path geology may never be understood except in a general way. It is not the purpose of this monograph to present a detailed review of earthquake ground motion characteristics but in order to discuss the influence of local soil conditions, a general summary of the influence of some of the other factors is required.

The variation of intensity of ground motions with distance from the source of energy release (plotted as attenuation curves) has been studied for many years. Plots of peak acceleration as a function of distance have been presented by numerous workers in the seismology and earthquake engineering fields as indicated by the partial listing in Table 1. While there has been reasonable agreement about the form of attenuation curves proposed by different workers for earthquakes with magnitudes of 6 to 7

TABLE 1. AVAILABLE EMPIRICAL RELATIONSHIPS: PEAK ACCELERATION

Gutenberg and Richter (1956)
Esteva and Rosenblueth (1964)
Blume (1965)
Housner (1965)
Kanai (1966)
Milne and Davenport (1969)
Seed, Idriss and Kiefer (1969)
Esteva (1970)
Cloud and Perez (1971)
Duke, Johnson, Larson and Engman (1972)
Page, Boore, Joyner and Coulter (1972)
Donovan (1973)
Schnabel and Seed (1973)
Esteva and Villaverde (1973)
McGuire (1974)
Orphal and Lahoud (1974)
Trifunac and Brady (1975)
Duke, Eguchi, Campbell and Chow (1976)
Seed, Murarka, Lysmer and Idriss (1976)
Trifunac (1976)
Blume (1977)
Ohashi, Iwasaki, Wakagayashi and Tokida (1977)
Ambraseys (1978)
Boore, Oliver, Page and Joyner (1978)
Bureau (1978)
Donovan and Bornstein (1978)
Faccioli (1978)
McGuire (1978)
Sadigh, Power and Youngs (1978)
Campbell (1981)
Joyner and Boore (1981)
Herrmann and Nuttli (1981)

and for distances of 25 to 60 kms, there have often been marked differences of opinion concerning accelerations in the near field and those developed by higher magnitude events. The main reason for these differences was the lack of data for near-field recording stations and for large magnitude events.

One of these deficiencies was remedied by the occurrence of the Imperial Valley earthquake of 1979 ($M_L \approx 6.5$). As shown in Fig. 14, the fault break in this earthquake extended some 35 km. from just south of the U.S.-Mexico border to just south of Brawley and a large number of instrument stations were located on both sides of the fault to record the motions (Porcella and Matthiesen, 1979). The records of this event provide the most complete source of near-field data ever obtained for the study of motion attenuation relationships. A plot of the variation of peak acceleration against closest distance to the source is shown in Fig. 15, together with the results of regression analyses to determine the mean and mean ± 1 standard deviation relationships for this data set. It may be seen that there is considerable scatter in the data, but a well-defined pattern is clearly recognizable, indicating a marked flattening of the slope of the curves within a few kilometers of the source. It should be noted that virtually all the recording stations for this earthquake were located on deposits of alluvium over several hundred feet in depth.

A similar attenuation relationship based on records of peak acceleration recorded only on rock is shown for similar magnitude earthquakes in Fig. 16. Although the near-field data for this data set are not so abundant as for the Imperial Valley data, it nevertheless defines an attenuation curve of similar shape.

Attenuation curves of this type for rock motions from different magnitude earthquakes have been determined by Seed and Schnabel (1980) and the resulting plots are shown in Fig. 17. Families of curves of this type can be used to estimate peak accelerations at different distances from different magnitude earthquakes. It may be noted in Fig. 17 that at very short distances from the source, peak accelerations are shown to be almost independent of earthquake magnitude for magnitudes greater than about $M_s = 6.5$. This result is indicated by the records of horizontal ground motions obtained to date, and

31

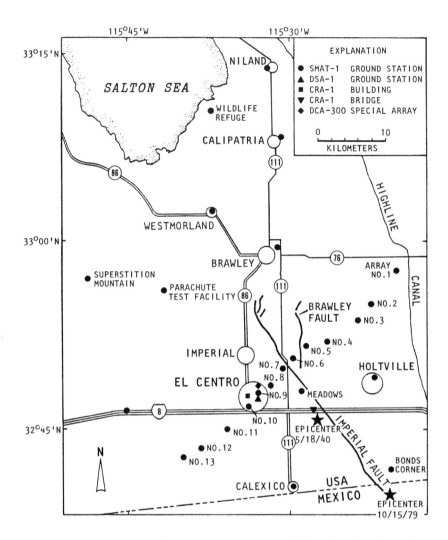

Figure 14. Strong-motion stations in the Imperial Valley, California (R.L. Porcella and R.B. Matthiesen, USGS Open-File Report 79–1654).

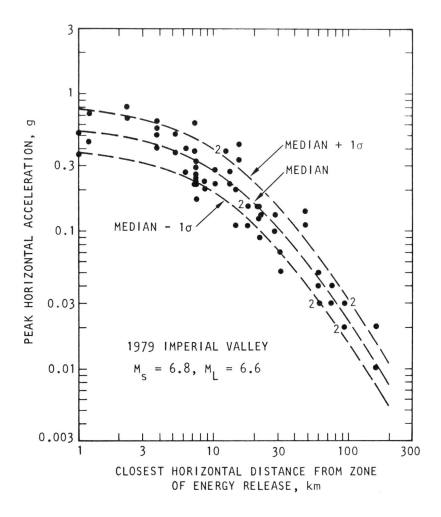

Figure 15. Regression analysis of the peak accelerations recorded during the October 15, 1979 Imperial Valley earthquake.

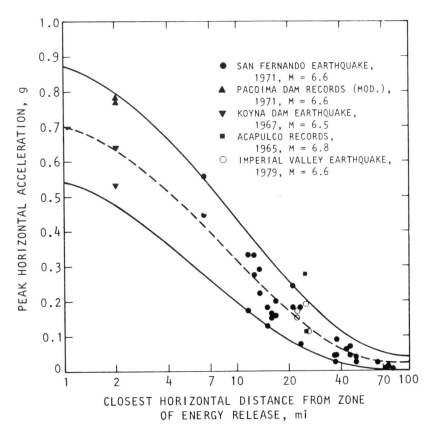

Figure 16. Maximum accelerations in rock for earthquakes with magnitude ≈ 6.6.

reflects the prevailing opinion among seismologists and earthquake engineers concerning near-field motions.

Influence of Soil Conditions on Ground Motion Characteristics

Peak Accelerations

The influence of soil conditions on peak ground accelerations can be determined by comparing the mean peak acceleration attenuation curve for deep soil deposits shown in Fig. 15 with that for accelerations recorded on rock sites shown in Fig. 16. This comparison in Fig. 18 indicates that at comparable distances from the source, peak accelerations recorded on rock are somewhat higher than those recorded on deep alluvium. More detailed studies, involving other earthquake records, show that this is typically the case for accelerations greater than about 0.1g. At lower acceleration levels, accelerations on deep soil deposits seem to be higher than those on rock.

The results of a detailed study of the relative values of peak accelerations developed on four different types of soil deposit:

1. Rock
2. Stiff soil deposits involving cohesionless soils or stiff clays to about 200 ft. in depth
3. Deep cohesionless soil deposits with depths greater than about 250 ft.
4. Deposits of soft to medium stiff clays and sands

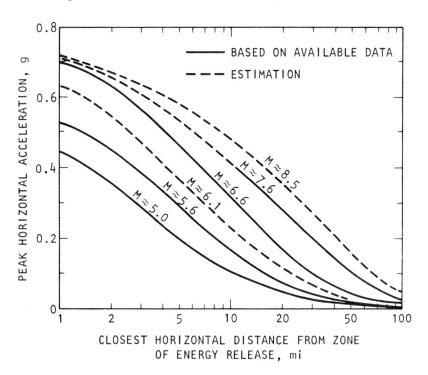

Figure 17. Average values of maximum accelerations in rock.

are shown in Fig. 19. It may be seen that apart from deposits involving soft to medium stiff clay, values of peak acceleration developed on different types of soil do not differ appreciably, particularly at acceleration levels less than about 0.3 to 0.4g. Even at high acceleration levels on rock of the order of 0.7g, accelerations on deposits of any depth which do not involve soft to medium stiff clays are likely to be only about 25% less than those on rock. Variations of this magnitude may not be significant in engineering practice and for most practical purposes it may well be considered that peak acceleration values on rock and stiff soils of any depth are about the same.

In fact, if data for all foundation conditions except soft to medium stiff clays are plotted together, it may not be possible to differentiate between acceleration levels for rock and differ-

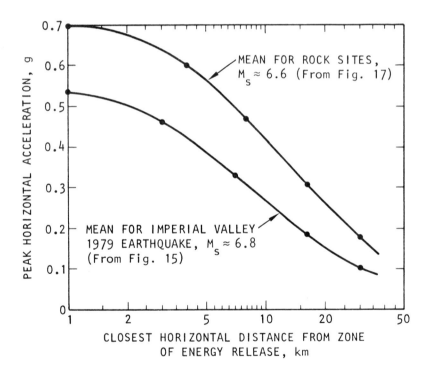

Figure 18. Comparison of attenuation curves for rock sites and Imperial Valley (1979) earthquake.

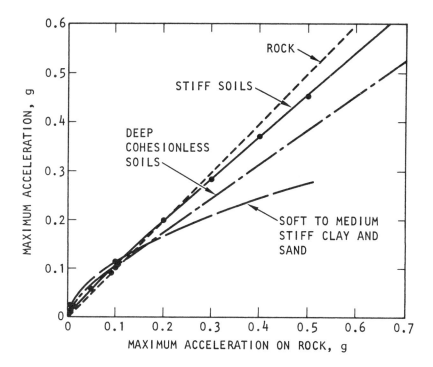

Figure 19. Approximate relationships between maximum accelerations on rock and other local site conditions.

ent site conditions. This has often been done and led to the conclusion that there is no significant influence of soil conditions on peak acceleration values. As shown in Fig. 19, this is generally so, though in detail some differentiation may be discerned.

In view of the large number of acceleration attenuation curves proposed over the past twenty years, it is important to recognize that with increasing availability of strong motion records and correspondingly less need for speculation on the probable levels of future motions, there has been an increasing degree of agreement on the forms of these curves. Typical of this development are the four acceleration attenuation curves shown in Fig. 20 for mean peak accelerations on stiff soil deposits due to magnitude $M_s = 7.5$ earthquakes. Variations between the curves developed by different investigators (Seed and Schnabel, 1980;

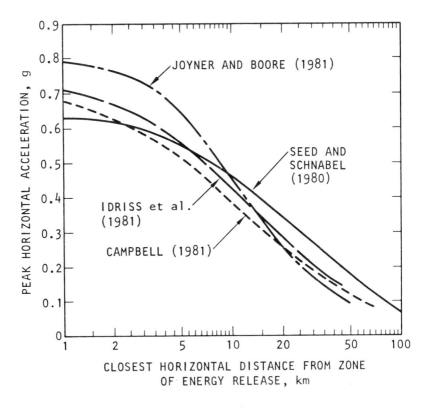

Figure 20. Peak ground acceleration curves for stiff soils ($M_s = 7.5$).

Idriss et al, 1981; Campbell, 1981; and Joyner and Boore, 1981) are relatively small compared with those evidenced by the earlier proposals.

It is interesting to compare the attenuation curves shown in Fig. 20, which are based largely on data from shallow-focus earthquakes and records obtained in the western part of the United States, with a comparably recent attenuation curve proposed by Nuttli and Herrmann (1981) for accelerations likely to develop in the eastern part of the United States, where earthquakes have large focal depths and the attenuation rate for ground motions is significantly less than in the western part of the country. This comparison is shown in Fig. 21, where it is seen that the relative positions of the curves are entirely consistent, with the deeper focus events producing lower accelerations at close distances and leading to higher accelerations at large distances due to the slower attenuation rate for the travel paths representative of eastern U.S. conditions.

Finally, it should be stressed that each of the attenuation curves shown in Figs. 17, 18 and 20 shows the mean value of acceleration and in reality represents a band of data with considerable scatter, similar to the results shown in Figs. 15 and 16. For critical structures it is sometimes desirable to determine acceleration values near the upper bound, say the 84th percentile value, as represented by the mean + 1 standard deviation curve in a statistical analysis of the scattered data points. Such a curve for the Imperial Valley (1979) earthquake data is shown in Fig. 15. From studies such as this it has been found that:

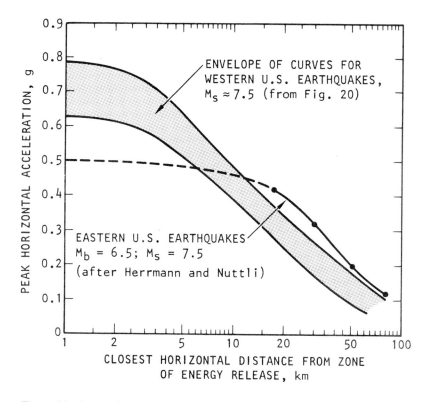

Figure 21. Comparison of attenuation curves for western and eastern U.S. earthquakes.

$$\frac{(a_{max})_{mean + 1}}{(a_{max})_{mean}} \approx 1.4 \text{ to } 1.5$$

This relationship provides a simple means of estimating the scatter of data points on either side of the mean curve and thereby assessing the desirable levels of peak acceleration for which different types of structures should be designed.

Maximum Ground Velocity

In the same way that peak acceleration data can be plotted to determine acceleration attenuation curves, values of peak velocity determined from recorded accelerograms can be plotted to determine velocity attenuation curves. A detailed study of such curves by Sadigh et al (1979) has led to the results shown in Fig. 22 for Magnitude $M_s \approx 6.5$ earthquakes and velocities recorded on rock and soil conditions. In this case it may be seen that the local soil conditions can have a pronounced effect on the peak velocity developed, with velocity values on soil deposits typically being about twice those recorded on rock sites.

By reading off mean values of peak acceleration (a_{max}) and mean values of maximum velocity (v_{max}) at equal distances from appropriate attenuation curves, it is possible to determine representative values for the ratio v_{max}/a_{max} for different site geologic conditions. While the values are found to vary to some extent with distance from the source, such studies have shown that for distances less than about 50 kms from the zone of energy release, representative average values of this ratio are approximately:

Geologic Condition	v_{max}/a_{max}
Rock	55 cm/sec/g
Stiff soils ($<$ 200$'$)	110 cm/sec/g
Deep stiff soils ($>$ 200$'$)	135 cm/sec/g

The significance of the ratio v_{max}/a_{max} was first noted by Newmark et al (1973) and the values of this ratio determined from more recent studies are in remarkably good agreement with values determined at that time.

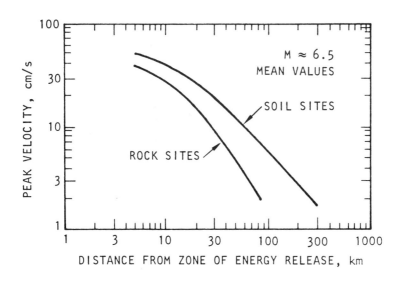

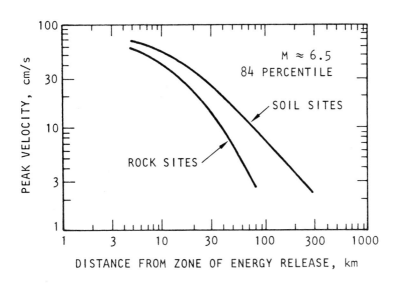

Figure 22. Variation of maximum ground velocity with distance for different site conditions (from Sadigh et al., 1979).

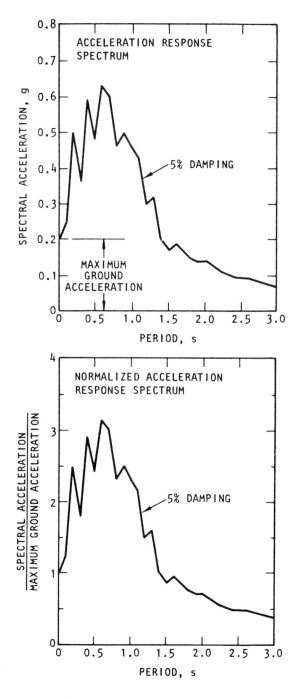

Figure 23. Determination of normalized acceleration response spectrum.

42

Response Spectra

Of the various characteristics of earthquake ground motions, none is so much influenced by the local soil conditions as the shape of the response spectrum. Since this is the most significant characteristic of an earthquake motion, it is mainly through their influence on this ground motion parameter that local conditions exert their significant influence on earthquake ground motions and therefore on potential building damage.

The spectral shape representative of any group of earthquake ground motion records is obtained by first determining the normalized acceleration response spectrum for each motion in the group. A normalized acceleration response spectrum is obtained by expressing the ordinates of a conventional spectrum as a proportion of the maximum ground acceleration for the motion for which the spectrum was derived, or the zero-period ordinate value, as shown in Fig. 23. For all normalized spectra, the zero period ordinate is therefore unity, and "mean" or "mean + 1 standard deviation" spectral shapes can readily be determined.

Studies of this type have been made for groups of accelerograph records obtained for the four different soil conditions previously discussed:

1. Rock sites
2. Stiff soil sites (less than 200 ft. deep)
3. Deep cohesionless soil sites (greater than 250 ft. deep)
4. Sites underlain by soft to medium stiff clay deposits.

While adequately large numbers of motions can be collected for soils in groups 1 to 3 above, there are relatively few strong motion records available for deposits of soft to medium stiff clay and, furthermore, the few available records show wide variations in characteristics. For such deposits, therefore, wide variations from the mean spectral shape should be expected.

Within this limitation the results of a study of the mean and 84-percentile spectral shapes for 5% damping and for the four different site conditions discussed above are shown in Figs. 24 and 25 respectively. It is readily apparent that there are wide differences in shapes depending on the soil conditions, par-

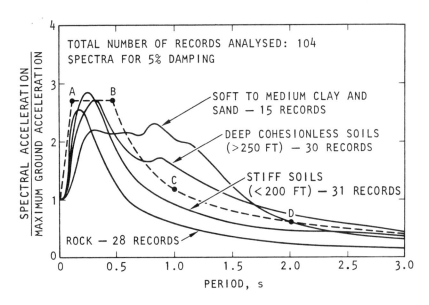

Figure 24. Average acceleration spectra for different site conditions.

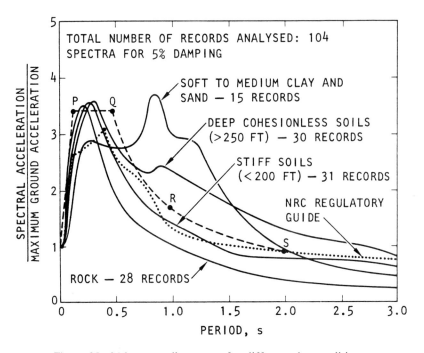

Figure 25. 84th percentile spectra for different site conditions.

44

ticularly at periods greater than about 0.5 second; above this value, spectral amplifications are much higher for deep cohesionless soil deposits and for soft to medium stiff clay deposits than for stiff soil conditions or rock. In other words, deep and soft deposits of soil introduce a significantly larger proportion of longer period components into the ground surface motions, the effects apparently increasing as the depth or softness of the soil increases. Failure to consider these effects for periods larger than about 0.5 second could lead to major discrepancies in evaluation of spectral accelerations or establishment of design criteria.

For engineering purposes it is often convenient and conservative to simplify the spectral shapes shown in Figs. 24 and 25. Thus, for example, in dealing with stiff soil or rock sites it is adequately conservative to represent the mean spectral shapes shown in Fig. 24 by the dotted line defined by the points A, B, C and D. The coordinates of these points are:

Point	Period	$(S_a)_{max} / a_{max}$
A	0.1 sec.	2.7
B	0.5 sec.	2.7
C	1.0 sec.	1.2
D	2.0 sec.	0.6

and, for 5% damping, the use of such a spectral shape would provide a conservative representation of the actual spectra. It may be noted that the maximum spectral acceleration, $(S_a)_{max}$, in this case is simply 2.7 times the maximum acceleration, a_{max}.

Similarly, in Fig. 25, for stiff soil and rock sites it is adequately conservative to represent the mean + 1 standard deviation spectral shape shown in Fig. 25 by the dotted line defined by the points P, Q, R and S. The coordinates of these points are:

Point	Period	$(S_a)_{max} / a_{max}$
P	0.1 sec.	3.4
Q	0.5 sec.	3.4
R	1.0 sec.	1.7
S	2.0 sec.	0.85

Again, for 5% damping, a curve of this shape would provide a conservative representation of the spectra shown in the figure. For such a curve the maximum spectral acceleration, $(S_a)_{max}$, is equal to 3.4 times the maximum acceleration, a_{max}, for the ground motion.

Finally it might be considered desirable for design purposes to simplify the response spectra shown in Fig. 24 for four different soil conditions to the form shown in Fig. 26, involving only three different categories of soil: rock and stiff soils; deep cohesionless soils; and soft to medium stiff clays and sands. Combining the curves shown in Fig. 26 with representative values of peak ground acceleration for the different soil types for an area where the maximum ground acceleration in rock might be 0.2g or more would lead to the relative spectral curves shown in Fig. 27. It may be noted that a similar family of curves has recently been recommended for use with national seismic design provisions, although in the interest of including greater conservatism for taller buildings and very low structures, the family of curves has been modified slightly as shown in Fig. 28 (Applied Technology Council, 1978).

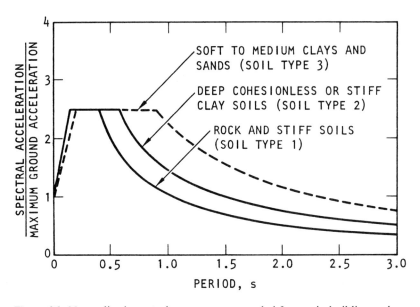

Figure 26. Normalized spectral curves recommended for use in building code.

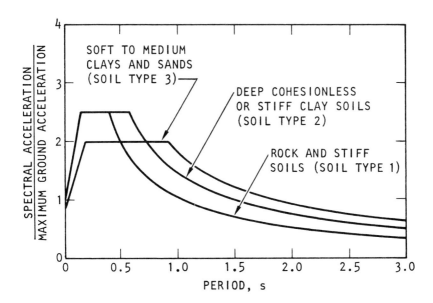

Figure 27. Spectral curves for use in building code normalized to EPA for stiff site conditions.

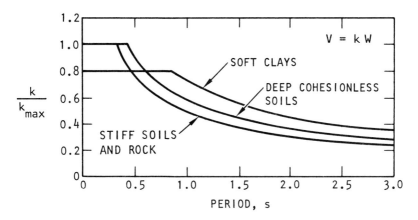

Figure 28. Proposed variation of lateral force coefficient for different soil conditions (tentative).

47

Selection of Ground Motions for Design

General Philosophy

In many cases the characteristics of the ground motions for which a structure should be designed can be specified in terms of a response spectrum, while in other cases it is desirable to specify a time history of accelerations. Whichever method is used to describe the earthquake motion, it is important to differentiate between two earthquake motions that are related but can be significantly different from each other:

1. The maximum free-field earthquake ground motions which a structure *should be able to withstand* with an acceptable margin of safety. These motions should reflect the seismic environment in which the structure is to be built and thus describe the maximum motions which the structure should be able to withstand without developing an unacceptably high level of damage. They might be called the "safety-level earthquake motions." They depend only on the seismicity of the region, the probability of occurrence of any level of ground motion within the life of the structure, and the risk which society is willing to accept with regard to the occurrence of the ground motions. They are not necessarily the same thing, however, as the design earthquake motions.

2. The level of shaking which should be incorporated into an analysis used by the engineer to guide him in evaluating the safety of a structure. This motion, which is often called the "design earthquake motion," depends on many factors, including the selected maximum free-field earthquake ground motions which the structure should be able to withstand, but it should also include consideration of such factors as:

   (a) Method of analysis into which it will be incorporated.

   (b) Conservatism of the analysis procedure.

   (c) Level of damping for which the analysis is being made, taking into account the acceptable level of damage.

48

(d) Depth of embedment of the structure in the ground and whether allowance is made in the design procedure for variations of ground motion with depth.

(e) Effects of soil-structure interaction, if they are not included directly in the analysis procedure.

(f) Effects of spatial variations in ground motions if they are not included directly in the analysis procedure.

(g) Material properties used in the analysis.

(h) Combination of loadings and/or components of ground motion used in the analysis.

(i) Strength characteristics of the structure and the consequences of transient stresses exceeding the strength of structural elements and members.

(j) Ductility of the structure.

(k) Acceptable level of damage.

This differentiation between the two earthquake motions is important, because the qualifications of individuals responsible for selecting the two motions are quite different. Establishment of the free-field motions that a structure should be designed to withstand requires a knowledge of seismic geology, seismology, strong ground motions and societal requirements. Selection of the design earthquake motions to be used in the engineering analysis requires a knowledge of strong motion ground response, material characteristics, analytical procedures, design procedures, and above all, experience relating the performance level of structures of different types during actual earthquakes with their design criteria.

In some cases, for example the evaluation of soil liquefaction potential using empirical procedures based on field observations, the two earthquake design motions may be the same; but in other cases, say involving the design of concrete structures using elastic response analyses, they can appropriately be quite different, the difference depending on the judgment of an experienced group of engineers. In fact, even for the same project, if it involves both earth and concrete structures, the design earthquake motions for the concrete structures may justifiably be different from those for the earth structures.

It is because of the diffcrence between the two motions, that is, the safety level earthquake motions and the design earthquake motions, that some earthquake-resistant design criteria appear to be less stringent than at first seems appropriate for the geologic and seismic environment in which a structure is to be built. A deeper insight and consideration of all the factors discussed above will show, however, that this is not the case and that reduced ground motion criteria are well-justified in the light of the conservatisms of the analysis and experience with known performance of structures.

Another desirable aspect of the design earthquake is that it should have a relatively smooth response spectrum so that there are no frequencies exhibiting low response characteristics. On the other hand, it is not essential that the motion be chosen in such a way that the spectrum envelops all conceivable spectral peaks that may actually occur. Design earthquakes are usually selected conservatively, and this approach, together with other conservatisms in design, provides adequate protection against the conceivable but often unlikely event of peak responses exceeding those corresponding to the design response spectra. For the same reasons, design spectra can safely be selected on the basis of generally representative levels of earthquake shaking and do not need to reflect the upper bounds of motions which might be contemplated by the most conservative of strong-motion researchers.

For normal structures it is generally considered adequately conservative to adopt free-field earthquake motions and spectra which are near the means of those indicated by the motion characteristics discussed in the previous section, while for critical structures design motions which are near the 84 percentile or mean + 1 standard deviation motion characteristics are amply conservative. There are various ways to obtain the mean + 1 standard deviation spectrum, but two of the most common are:

1. Use an acceleration value near the mean value of maximum acceleration as the anchor point for a mean + 1 standard deviation spectral shape, or

2. Use an acceleration value near the mean + 1 standard deviation value of peak acceleration as the anchor point for a mean spectral shape.

It would usually be unreasonably conservative to use a mean + 1 standard deviation value of peak acceleration as anchor point for a mean + 1 standard deviation spectral shape since this would be tantamount to using a mean + 2 standard deviation spectrum. However, judgments on these issues require a knowledge of all other aspects of the design and cannot be prescribed as blanket rules.

Specification of Design Spectra

For the design of many steel and concrete structures it is often found most desirable to specify the response spectrum for the free-field motions and, if a time history of acceleration is required for some aspects of the analysis, to develop a time history which has

(a) the general characteristics of a reasonable earthquake motion, and
(b) a response spectrum that just envelops the specified spectrum shape.

In many cases the analysis can be made directly from the spectrum and a time history of accelerations is not required.

In developing design criteria such as maximum ground acceleration a_{max}, maximum ground velocity v_{max}, maximum spectral acceleration $(S_a)_{max}$ and the shape of spectral curves, several simple guidelines previously discussed may be used. Thus:

1. Once the magnitude and distance to the source of energy release of possible earthquakes have been determined, values of the mean peak acceleration may be read off directly from curves such as those in Fig. 17.
2. Peak accelerations for different soil conditions may be obtained by correcting the mean peak accelerations for rock sites to mean peak accelerations for other sites using curves such as those in Fig. 19 or they may be read off directly from curves such as those shown in Figs. 20 and 21.
3. Values of mean + 1 standard deviation peak acceleration can be determined from the relationship

51

$$\frac{(a_{max})_{mean + 1}}{(a_{max})_{mean}} \approx 1.4 \text{ to } 1.5$$

4. For sites within about 50 kms. of the causative fault, values of maximum ground velocity can be obtained from the relationships

For rock sites : $v_{max}/a_{max} \approx 55 \text{ cm/sec/g}$

For stiff soils : $v_{max}/a_{max} \approx 110 \text{ cm/sec/g}$

5. Values of maximum spectral acceleration may be obtained from the relationships

For mean spectral shape : $(S_a)_{max} \approx 2.7 \, a_{max}$

For mean + 1 spectral shape : $(S_a)_{max} \approx 3.4 \, a_{max}$

6. The shapes of conservative response spectra for rock and stiff soils sites can be defined by the coordinates of points ABCD in Fig. 24 or points PQRS in Fig. 25.

The applicability of these guidelines may be illustrated by applying them to develop design free-field motion spectra for the LNG Terminal to be constructed on a stiff soil site at Point Conception, California—a structure for which seismic design criteria were recently recommended by a Seismic Review Panel (1981). The Panel concluded that the "largest rationally conceivable earthquakes" which could affect this site were either a Magnitude 6¾ event occurring 5 kms. from the site or a Magnitude 7½ event occurring 12 kms. from the site. Following the steps listed as 1 to 5 above leads to the following values:

Earthquake Magnitude:	6¾	7½
Distance of site from source:	5 km	12 km
$(a_{max})_{Mean}$ for rock—from Fig. 17:	0.57g	0.46g
$(a_{max})_{Mean}$ for stiff soil—from Fig. 19:	0.51g	0.43g
$(a_{max})_{M + 1} = 1.45 \, (a_{max})_{Mean}$:	0.74g	0.63g
$(v_{max})_{M + 1} = 110 \, (a_{max})_{M + 1}$:	82 cm/sec	70 cm/sec
$(S_a)_{max} = 2.7 \, (a_{max})_{M + 1}$:	2.0g	1.7g
$(S_a)_{max} = 3.4 \, (a_{max})_{Mean}$:	1.75g	1.5g

A comparison of the design earthquake characteristics obtained in this way with those recommended by the Seismic Review Panel is shown below:

	Design Values	
	From above procedure	Recommended by Panel
Max. acceleration	0.74g	0.75g
Max. velocity	82 cm / sec	85 cm / sec
Max. Spectral Acceleration	1.5 to 2.0g	1.75g

and a comparison of the design spectrum recommended by the Panel with that defined by the points ABCD and PQRS in Figs. 24 and 25 is shown in Fig. 29. The reasonable agreement is apparent.

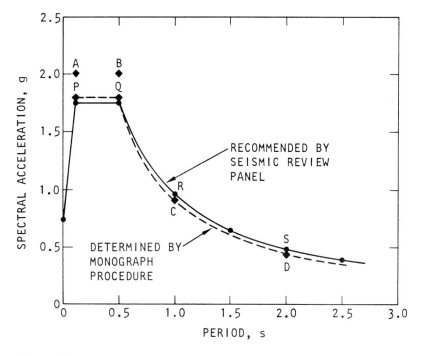

Figure 29. Comparision of design spectra for largest rationally conceivable earthquakes affecting LNG facility at Point Conception, California.

It is not meant to suggest by this example that the Seismic Review Panel for this project arrived at its recommendations following the procedure outlined here. The results are presented only to illustrate a possible procedure that leads to results similar to those recommended by experienced engineers and geologists. Similar examples could readily have been drawn from the records of other projects involving critical structures in California. It should be emphasized, however, that various aspects of the design earthquake and similar levels of motion may not be applicable to other projects even though the magnitudes and locations of the earthquake sources are comparable.

Specification of Design Accelerograms

For some purposes, such as the earthquake-resistant design of earth dams, it has been found more appropriate to specify design earthquake criteria in the form of accelerograms rather than design spectra. The selection of suitable accelerograms is based on the same general principles as those governing the selection of response spectra. Customarily, the accelerograms used are modified forms of recorded motions, the modifications being made to change the predominant period, to change the acceleration levels, to extend the duration, or to fill in significant dips in the response spectrum. When design accelerograms are specified, usually two or more time histories are used to ensure that no significant combination of frequencies affecting the response is overlooked.

A typical example of the use of a modified earthquake record for design purposes is shown in Fig. 30 (after Wahler and Associates, 1981). This record, which is a modified form of the motions recorded at the Castaic Station in southern California during the San Fernando earthquake of 1971 (Magnitude $\approx$ 6.5) was selected for the evaluation of seismic stability of Camanche Dam, located 30 miles east of San Francisco. The maximum credible earthquake motions to which the dam might be subjected were determined to result from the possibility of a Magnitude 6½ earthquake occurring on the Bear Mountain Fault about 10 miles from the dam site, and the main characteristics of the design accelerogram were selected to be:

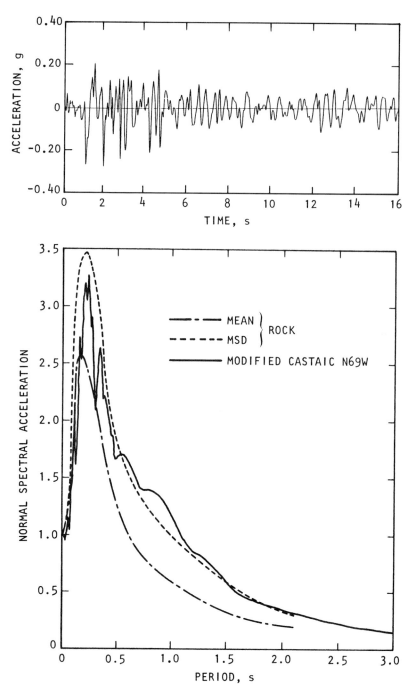

Figure 30. Design accelerogram and spectrum for Camanche Dam (After Wahler and Assoc., 1981).

1. A peak acceleration of 0.33g
2. Response spectrum close to the mean + 1 standard deviation spectrum shape for rock records, and
3. A duration of about 16 seconds.

The spectrum for the Castaic record as modified to meet these characteristics is shown in the lower part of Fig. 30. Modification of existing records in this way is often used for evaluating the seismic stability of earth dams.

Conclusions

The preceding pages have emphasized the role of local soil conditions in determining the characteristics of earthquake ground motions to be used in engineering design. Other factors also influence these motions and, to the extent possible, these factors should be given due consideration in selecting the free-field motions for which a structure should be designed. The selection of design motions can best be accomplished by the cooperative efforts of geologists, seismologists and engineers; each has a major role to play in arriving at a decision concerning this critical aspect of earthquake-resistant design.

Soil Liquefaction

Introduction

One of the most dramatic causes of damage to structures during earthquakes has been the development of liquefaction in saturated sand deposits, manifested either by the formation of boils and mud-spouts at the ground surface, by seepage of water through ground cracks or in some cases by the development of quick-sand-like conditions over substantial areas. Where the latter phenomenon occurs, buildings may sink substantially into the ground or tilt excessively, light-weight structures may float upwards to the ground surface and foundations may displace laterally causing structural failures.

While liquefaction has been reported in numerous earthquakes (Seed, 1968), nowhere has the phenomenon been more dramatically illustrated in recent years than in the Niigata, Japan earthquake of 1964 and the Alaska earthquake the same year. Much can be learned from an examination of soil behavior in these two events. The results of field studies following these earthquakes are summarized below.

Liquefaction Effects in the Niigata Earthquake of June 16, 1964

Although the epicenter of the Niigata earthquake (Magnitude ≈ 7.5) was located about 35 miles from Niigata and the maximum ground accelerations recorded in the city were about 0.16g, the earthquake induced extensive liquefaction in the low-lying areas of the city. Water began to flow out of cracks and boils during and immediately following the earthquake, as shown in Fig. 31, causing liquefaction of the deposits and widespread damage. Many structures settled more than 3 ft. in the liquefied soil and the settlement was often accompanied by severe tilting, as shown in Fig. 3. Thousands of buildings collapsed or suffered major damage as a result of these effects (Ohsaki, 1966).

The city is underlain by a deep deposit of sand with a 50 percent size ranging from about 0.2 to 0.4 mm and a uniformity

Figure 31. Initial stages of water flow from ground, Niigata (1964).

coefficient of about 10. Following the earthquake an extensive survey of the distribution of the damaged structures was made. It was found that structures in the coastal dune area (designated Zone A) suffered practically no damage. The major damage and evidences of liquefaction were concentrated in the lowland areas but even here, two distinct zones could be clearly recognized—one in which damage and liquefaction were extensive (Zone C) and one in which damage was relatively light (Zone B). Because all zones contained similar types of structures, the differences in extent of damage could be attributed to differences in the subsoil and foundation behavior. Studies were conducted by a number of Japanese engineers to determine the differences in soil conditions in the various zones.

The difference in behavior in Zone A from that in Zones B and C could readily be attributed to two major differences in soil characteristics. Although all zones were underlain by sandy soils to a depth of approximately 100 ft., in Zone A the underlying sands were considerably denser than those in Zones B and C and, furthermore, the water table was at a much greater depth below the ground surface. In Zones B and C, however, the general topography and depth of water table was essentially the same. It was therefore concluded that the difference in extent of damage in these two zones must be related to the characteristics of the underlying sands. Accordingly, considerable effort was made to determine any significant differences in the general soil conditions in those zones.

Because the soils involved are sands, efforts were concentrated on the determination of the relative density of the sands by means of standard penetration tests. Koizumi (1966) has presented the results of a number of borings made in Zones B and C to show the variation of penetration resistance with depth in the two zones. There is a considerable scatter of the results in any one zone, but averaging the values obtained leads to the comparative values shown in Fig. 32(a).

It may be seen that in Zones B and C, the average penetration resistance of the sands is essentially the same in the top 15 ft. Below this the sands in Zone B are somewhat denser than those in Zone C. Below about 45 ft., the sands in both zones are relatively dense and are unlikely to be involved in liquefaction. It

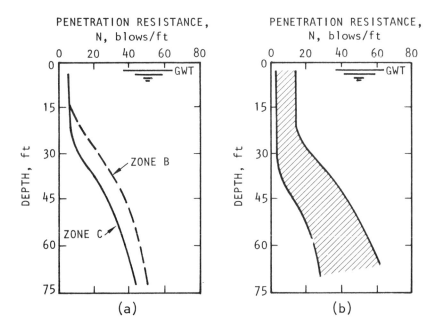

Figure 32. Standard penetration resistance of Niigata Sands.

seems reasonable to conclude that the relatively small differences in penetration resistance of the sands in the depth range from 15 ft. to 45 ft. are responsible for the major difference in foundation and liquefaction behavior in the two zones.

In addition to comparing the soil conditions in the different damage zones, Japanese engineers have made a detailed study of the relationship between soil and foundation conditions and building performance in Zone C. Here the variation of penetration resistance with depth falls within the shaded area shown in Fig. 32 (b), the standard penetration resistance in the top 25 ft. generally being less than 15, but sometimes falling as low as 5. For each building in this zone, the extent of damage caused by foundation failure was classified into one of four categories ranging from the no-damage category I (buildings that settled up to 8″ or tilted up to 20 minutes of angle) to the heavy damage category IV (buildings settling more than 3′ or tilting more than 2.3°).

A study was made of the influence of foundation type on the settlement and tilting of reinforced concrete buildings in Zone C (Kishida, 1966). Some of these buildings had shallow spread footing foundations; others were supported on short piles, typically extending to a depth of about 25 ft. For each foundation type, the proportion of buildings in the light damage categories I and II was compared with the proportion in the heavy damage categories III and IV. The results of this comparison are shown in Table 2, from which it may be seen that the provision of short pile foundations apparently had little effect in reducing the damage caused by the earthquake ground motions.

TABLE 2. Influence of Type of Foundation on Extent of Damage

Type of Foundation	No Damage and Slight Damage	Intermediate and Heavy Damage
Shallow (63 buildings)	36%	64%
Pile (122 buildings)	45%	55%

For buildings with spread footing foundations, a study was made to determine the relationship between the penetration resistance of the sand at the base of the foundation and the extent of damage. The results of this study are shown in Fig. 33.

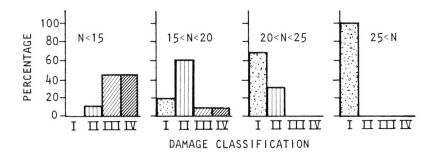

Figure 33. Relationship between penetration resistance at base of foundation and extent of damage.

When the sand underlying the footings had a penetration resistance of less than 15, the buildings usually suffered heavy damage (categories III and IV). However, when the penetration resistance was between 20 and 25, the structures suffered only light damage, or none. Thus it appears that a penetration resistance of slightly more than 20 would be adequate to prevent foundation settlements exceeding about 8″ in this earthquake.

The results of a similar study to determine the relationship between depth of piles, penetration resistance of the sand at the pile tip, and the extent of damage for pile-supported structures, are shown in Fig. 34. From these data it may be seen that for pile lengths varying from 15 to 60 ft., generally heavy damage (large settlements and tilting, or both) occurred when the penetration resistance of the sand at the pile tip was less than 15. However, for the same range of pile lengths, settlements and tilting were generally small when the penetration resistance of the sand at the pile tip exceeded 25. Thus the penetration resistance values providing satisfactory performance for pile foundations are quite similar to those providing satisfactory performance for footing foundations.

Finally, for a wide range of buildings and conditions in the heavy damage area, studies were made by Kishida, Koizumi and Ohsaki to establish the penetration resistance values at different depths which separated liquefiable from non-liquefiable soil conditions. The results of these studies are shown in Fig. 35. It may be seen that the desirable value of penetration resistance increases with depth, but the boundary values resulting from the three studies are reasonably consistent.

These results provide a valuable guide in assessing the liquefaction potential of other sand deposits, though it should be noted that they are only relevant directly to the soil, ground water and ground motion conditions existing in Niigata in the 1964 earthquake.

Liquefaction Effects in the Alaska Earthquake of April 29, 1964

The major effects of liquefaction in the Alaska earthquake (Magnitude ≈ 8.3) were massive landslides in the cities of Anchorage, Seward, Valdez and around the borders of Kenai Lake

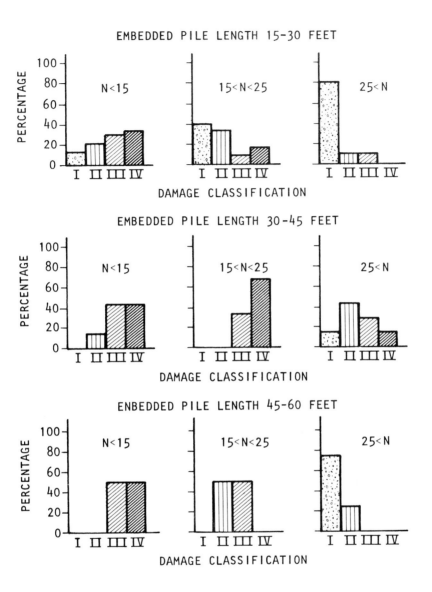

Figure 34. Influence of penetration resistance at tip of piles on extent of damage.

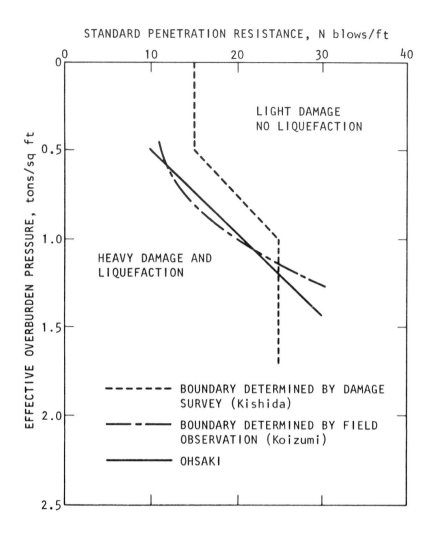

Figure 35. Analysis of liquefaction potential at Niigata for earthquake of June 16, 1964.

(Seed, 1968). The landslide at Valdez led to a decision to relocate the entire town on better foundation conditions several miles away; damage in Seward and Anchorage was catastrophic. A discussion of landslides, however, is outside the scope of this monograph, which is concerned only with soil liquefaction on relatively level ground and its influence on the foundations of structures.

In this regard, one of the most interesting effects of the Alaska earthquake was the extensive damage it caused to a wide variety of bridge foundations located at distances of 50 to 80 miles from the zone of major energy release (Ross, Seed, and Migliaccio, 1969). Damage included horizontal movement of abutment foundations toward stream channels, spreading and settlement of abutment fills, horizontal displacements and tilting of piers, and severe differential settlements of abutments and piers.

The greatest concentrations of severe damage occurred in regions characterized by thick deposits of saturated cohesionless soils. Ample evidence exists of liquefaction of these materials during the earthquake, and this phenomenon probably played a major role in the development of foundation displacements and bridge damage. Typical foundation conditions in these areas consisted of piles driven through saturated sands and silts of low to medium relative density (standard penetration resistance less than about 20 to 25); of approximately 60 samples investigated from the heavy damage area, two-thirds of the samples had a 10 percent size ranging from about 0.01 to 0.1 mm and a uniformity coefficient of 2 to 4. On the other hand, bridges supported on gravels and gravelly sands regardless of their penetration resistance values, generally showed small or no displacements, indicating no significant liquefaction of these materials under comparable conditions.

Causes of Soil Liquefaction

The basic cause of liquefaction of sands has been understood, in a qualitative way, for many years. If a saturated sand is subjected to ground vibrations, it tends to compact and decrease in volume; if drainage is unable to occur, the tendency to decrease

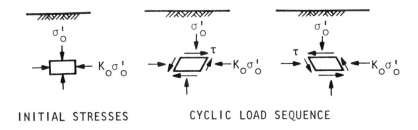

INITIAL STRESSES   CYCLIC LOAD SEQUENCE

(a)   Idealized field loading conditions

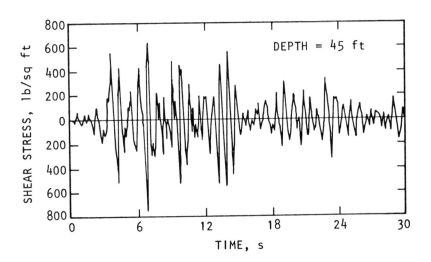

(b)   Shear stress variation determined by
response analysis

Figure 36. Cyclic shear stresses on a soil element during ground shaking.

66

in volume results in an increase in pore water pressure, and if the pore water pressure builds up to the point at which it is equal to the overburden pressure, the effective stress becomes zero, the sand loses its strength completely, and it develops a liquefied state.

In more quantitative terms, it is now generally believed that the basic cause of liquefaction in saturated cohesionless soils during earthquakes is the buildup of excess hydrostatic pressure due to the application of cyclic shear stresses induced by the ground motions. These stresses are generally considered to be due primarily to upward propagation of shear waves in a soil deposit, although other forms of wave motions are also expected to occur. Thus, soil elements can be considered to undergo a series of cyclic stress conditions as illustrated in Fig. 36, the stress series being somewhat random in pattern but nevertheless cyclic in nature.

As a consequence of the applied cyclic stresses, the structure of the cohesionless soil tends to become more compact with a resulting transfer of stress to the pore water and a reduction in stress on the soil grains. As a result, the soil grain structure rebounds to the extent required to keep the volume constant, and this interplay of volume reduction and soil structure rebound determines the magnitude of the increase in pore water pressure in the soil (Martin et al, 1975). The basic phenomenon is illustrated schematically in Fig. 37. The mechanism can be quantified so that the pore pressure increases due to any given sequence of stress applications can be computed from a knowledge of the stress-strain characteristics, the volume change characteristics of the sand under cyclic strain conditions, and the rebound characteristics of the sand due to stress reduction.

As the pore water pressure approaches a value equal to the applied confining pressure, the sand begins to undergo deformations. If the sand is loose, the pore pressure will increase suddenly to a value equal to the applied confining pressure, and the sand will rapidly begin to undergo large deformations with shear strains that may exceed ± 20 percent or more. If the sand will undergo virtually unlimited deformations without mobilizing significant resistance to deformation, it can be said to be liquefied. If, on the other hand, the sand is dense, it may develop

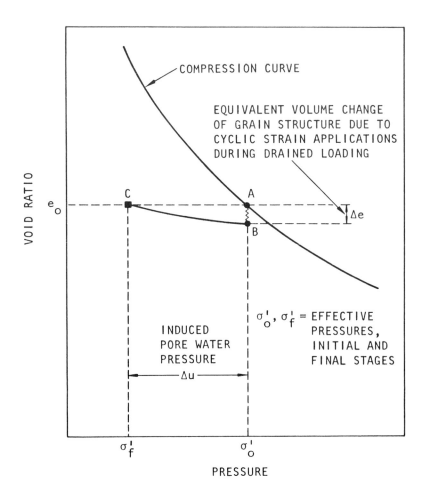

Figure 37. Schematic illustration of mechanism of pore pressure generation during cyclic loading.

a residual pore water pressure, on completion of a full stress cycle, which is equal to the confining pressure (a peak cyclic pore pressure ratio of 100%), but when the cyclic stress is reapplied on the next stress cycle, or if the sand is subjected to monotonic loading, the soil will tend to dilate, the pore pressure will drop if the sand is undrained, and the soil will ultimately develop enough resistance to withstand the applied stress. However, it will have to undergo some degree of deformation to develop the resistance, and as the cyclic loading continues, the amount of deformation required to produce a stable condition may increase. Ultimately, however, for any cyclic loading condition, there appears to be a cyclic strain level at which the soil will be able to withstand any number of cycles of a given stress without further increase in maximum deformation (De Alba et al, 1976). This type of behavior is termed "cyclic mobility" and it is considerably less serious than liquefaction, its significance depending on the magnitude of the limiting strain. It should be noted, however, that once the cyclic stress applications stop, if they return to a zero stress condition, there will be a residual pore water pressure in the soil equal to the overburden pressure, and this will inevitably lead to an upward flow of water in the soil which could have deleterious consequences for overlying layers.

Liquefaction of a sand in this way may develop in any zone of a deposit where the necessary combination of in-situ conditions and vibratory deformations may occur. Such a zone may be at the surface or at some depth below the ground surface, depending only on the state of the sand and the induced motions.

However, liquefaction of the upper layers of a deposit may also occur, not as a direct result of the ground motions to which they are subjected, but because of the development of liquefaction in an underlying zone of the deposit. Once liquefaction develops at a some depth in a mass of sand, the excess hydrostatic pressures in the liquefied zone will dissipate by flow of water in an upward direction. If the hydraulic gradient becomes sufficiently large, the upward flow of water will induce a "quick" or liquefied condition in the surface layers of the deposit. Liquefaction of this type will depend on the extent to which the necessary hydraulic gradient can be developed and maintained;

this, in turn, will be determined by the compaction characteristics of the sand, the nature of ground deformations, the permeability of the sand, the boundary drainage conditions, the geometry of the particular situation, and the duration of the induced vibrations.

It is now possible to analyze the generation and dissipation of pore water pressures in soil deposits during and following earthquakes (Finn et al, 1977; Liou et al, 1977; Martin and Seed, 1979; Seed et al, 1976), and the results of such studies can provide valuable insights into possible site behavior in some cases. However, the level of analytical capability used in these studies has probably outstretched our engineering ability to provide details of soil profile stratification and soil property determinations with sufficient accuracy to make the analytical results reliable. Furthermore, in dealing with sands, silty sands and silts, for which most liquefaction problems occur, dissipation effects during an earthquake are not significant. Accordingly it is customary to base evaluations of soil liquefaction or cyclic mobility potential on the assumption that all sand layers are undrained during the period of earthquake shaking. If under undrained conditions, it can be shown that every layer in a soil profile has an adequate margin of safety against the development of liquefaction or cyclic mobility, then no significant pore pressures will be generated and consideration of pore pressure dissipation is unnecessary. This approach is followed in the procedures outlined in the following pages for evaluating the liquefaction potential of soil deposits.

General Method of Evaluating Liquefaction Potential

The liquefaction potential of any given soil deposit is determined by a combination of the soil properties, environmental factors and characteristics of the earthquake to which it may be subjected. Specific factors which any liquefaction evaluation should desirably take into account include the following:

Soil Properties:
    Dynamic shear modulus
    Damping characteristics

Unit weight
Grain characteristics
Relative density
Soil structure
Environmental Factors:
Method of soil formation
Seismic history
Geologic history (aging, cementation)
Lateral earth pressure coefficient
Depth of water table
Effective confining pressure
Earthquake Characteristics:
Intensity of ground shaking
Duration of ground shaking

Some of these factors cannot be determined directly, but their effects can be included in the evaluation procedure by performing cyclic loading tests on undisturbed samples or by measuring the liquefaction characteristics of the soil by means of some in-situ test procedure. With due recognition of this fact, the basic evaluation procedure involves:

1. A determination of the cyclic shear stresses induced by the earthquake ground motions at different depths in the deposit and conversion of the irregular stress histories to equivalent numbers of uniform stress cycles. By this means the intensity of ground shaking, the duration of shaking, and the variations of induced shear stresses with depth are taken into account. The determination may be made either by a ground response analysis (involving the unit weight of the soils, the dynamic moduli and the soil damping characteristics) or by a simplified computational procedure described later. In either case, it should lead to a plot of the induced equivalent uniform shear stress level as a function of depth as shown in Fig. 38.

2. A determination, by means of laboratory cyclic loading tests on representative undisturbed samples conducted at different confining pressures, or by correlation of these properties

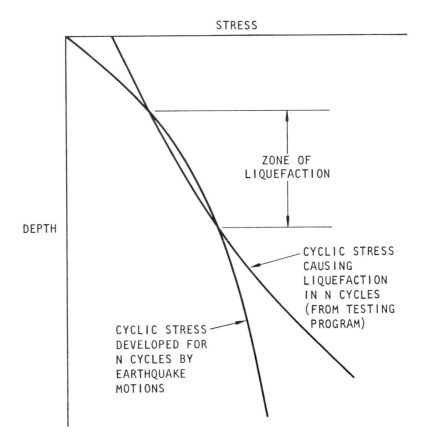

Figure 38. Method of evaluating liquefaction potential.

with some measurable in-situ characteristics, of the cyclic shear stresses that would have to be developed at various depths in order to cause liquefaction to occur in the same number of stress cycles as that determined in Step 1 to be representative of the particular earthquake under consideration. Either cyclic load simple shear tests or cyclic load triaxial compression tests may be used for this purpose, provided the test results are appropriately corrected to be representative of field loading conditions. By this means the soil type, the in-place conditions, the seismic and geologic histories of the deposit, and the initial effective stress conditions are appropriately taken into acount. The stresses required to cause liquefaction can then be plotted as a function of depth as shown in Fig. 38.

3. A comparison of the shear stresses induced by the earthquake with those required to cause liquefaction, to determine whether any zone exists within the deposit where liquefaction can be expected to occur, that is, where induced stresses exceed those required to cause liquefaction.

In applying the method, different procedures may be used to conduct the ground response analysis, and consideration may be given to performing the analysis in steps to take into account the changing deformation characteristics of the soil as the pore pressures build up. In most cases this latter refinement is unnecessary since the soil properties do not change appreciably until liquefaction is imminent. Even so, a ground response analysis may involve techniques, skills and equipment that are not readily available. In addition, the conduct and interpretation of cyclic load tests may present difficulties.

In applying the method over a period of time, simplified techniques have been developed for evaluating induced stresses and soil liquefaction characteristics which are sufficiently accurate for many practical purposes and circumvent some of the problems associated with interpretation of laboratory test data. These techniques are described in the following pages.

Simplified Procedure for Evaluating Stresses
Induced by Earthquakes

The shear stresses developed at any point in a soil deposit during an earthquake appear to be due primarily to the vertical propagation of shear waves in the deposit. This leads to a simplified procedure for evaluating the induced shear stresses (Seed and Idriss, 1971). If the soil column above a soil element at depth h behaved as a rigid body, the maximum shear stress on the soil element would be

$$(\tau_{max})_r = \frac{\gamma h}{g} \cdot a_{max} \tag{1}$$

where a_{max} is the maximum ground surface acceleration and γ is the unit weight of the soil; see Fig. 39(a). Because the soil column behaves as a deformable body, the actual shear stress at depth h, $(\tau_{max})_d$, as determined by a ground response analysis will be less than $(\tau_{max})_r$ and might be expressed by

$$(\tau_{max})_d = r_d \cdot (\tau_{max})_r \tag{2}$$

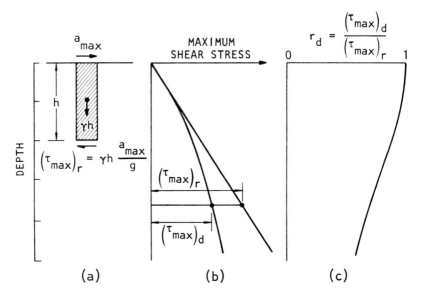

Figure 39. Procedure for determining maximum shear stress, $(\tau_{max})_r$.

74

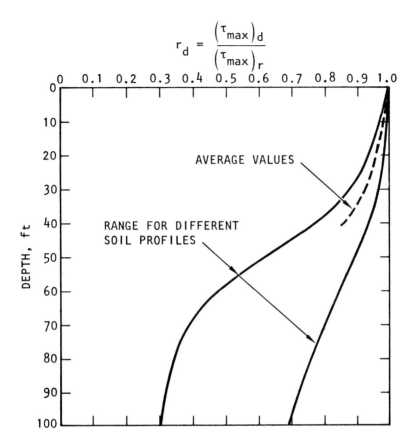

$$r_d = \frac{(\tau_{max})_d}{(\tau_{max})_r}$$

Figure 40. Range of values of r_d for different soil profiles.

where r_d is a stress reduction coefficient with a value less than 1. The variations of $(\tau_{max})_r$ and $(\tau_{max})_d$ will typically have the form shown in Fig. 39(b) and, in any given deposit, the value of r_d will decrease from a value of 1 at the ground surface to much lower values at large depths, as shown in Fig. 39(c).

Computations of the value of r_d for a wide variety of earthquake motions and soil conditions having sand in the upper 50 ft. have shown that r_d generally falls within the range of values shown in Fig. 40. It may be seen that in the upper 30 or 40 ft., the scatter of the results is not great and, for any of the deposits, the error involved in using the average values shown by the dashed line would generally be less than about 5%. Thus

75

to depths of about 40 ft., a reasonably accurate assessment of the maximum shear stress developed during an earthquake can be made from the relationship

$$\tau_{max} = \frac{\gamma h}{g} \cdot a_{max} \cdot r_d \tag{3}$$

where values of r_d are taken from the dashed line in Fig. 40. The critical depth for development of liquefaction, if it is going to occur, will normally be in the depth covered by this relationship.

The actual time history of shear stress at any point in a soil deposit during an earthquake will have an irregular form such as that shown in Fig. 41. From such relationships it is necessary to determine the equivalent uniform average shear stress. By appropriate weighting of the individual stress cycles, based on laboratory test data, this determination can readily be made. However, after making these determinations for a number of different cases it has been found that with a reasonable degree of accuracy, the average equivalent uniform shear stress, τ_{av}, is about 65% of the maximum shear stress, τ_{max}. Combining this result with the above expression for τ_{max} it follows that for practical purposes, the average cyclic shear stress may be determined by:

$$\tau_{av} \approx 0.65 \cdot \frac{\gamma h}{g} \cdot a_{max} \cdot r_d \tag{4}$$

The appropriate number of significant stress cycles N_c will depend on the duration of ground shaking and thus on the

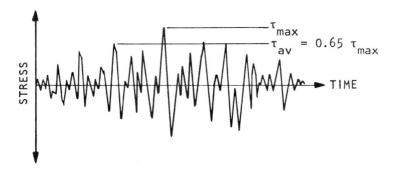

Figure 41. Time history of shear stresses during earthquake.

76

magnitude of the earthquake. Representative numbers of stress cycles are as follows:

Earthquake Magnitude	No. of Significant Stress Cycles, N_c
5¼	2–3
6	5
6¾	10
7½	15
8½	26

The use of these values together with stresses determined from Eq. 4 provides a simple procedure for evaluating the stresses induced at different depths by any given earthquake for which the maximum ground surface acceleration is known.

Determination of Cyclic Stress Levels Causing Liquefaction From Laboratory Test Data

Cyclic Simple Shear Tests

The most desirable laboratory test procedure for reproducing the effects of an earthquake on soil test samples is a cyclic loading simple shear test or torsional shear test. This procedure provides a reasonably close simulation of the stresses induced on a soil element by one component of earthquake motion in the field.

Typical results of a cyclic simple shear test on a sample of loose sand are shown in Fig. 42. In the early stages of cyclic stress applications, pore water pressures build up in the sample but there is no significant deformation. After a number of applications, the pore pressure suddenly jumps to a value equal to the vertical confining pressure, reducing the effective pressure to zero and at the same time the sample begins to undergo large cyclic deformations. This denotes the onset of liquefaction.

The number of stress cycles required to cause the sample to liquefy depends on the magnitudes of the applied shear stress and the initial vertical effective pressure under which the sample is consolidated. Typical results of a series of tests on identical

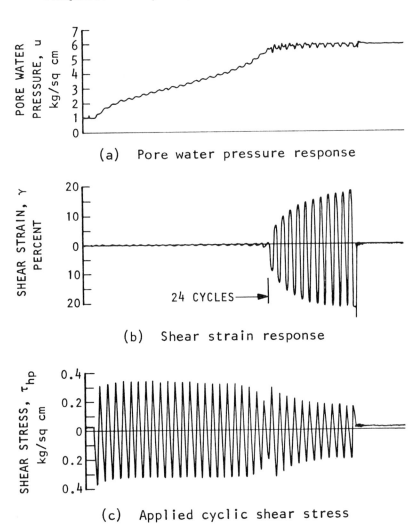

LOOSE MONTEREY SAND

INITIAL RELATIVE DENSITY, $D_r \approx 50\%$

INITIAL VOID RATIO, $e_i = 0.68$

INITIAL CONFINING PRESSURE, $\sigma_v = 5.0$ kg per sq cm

FREQUENCY = 1 cycle per second

(a) Pore water pressure response

24 CYCLES

(b) Shear strain response

(c) Applied cyclic shear stress

Figure 42. Record of a typical cyclic loading test on loose sand—simple shear conditions.

78

samples of sand at a relative density of 50% are shown in Fig. 43. From plots of this type it is readily possible to read off the cyclic shear stress ratio, τ_h / σ_v', causing liquefaction in the number of stress cycles representative of the design earthquake.

When tests are performed on dense samples of sand, the onset of liquefaction or cyclic mobility is not so abrupt and a critical condition is normally considered to develop when the pore pressure ratio builds up to a value of 100% and the cyclic shear strain is ± 5%.

Studies have been conducted to determine the difference in stresses causing liquefaction for simple shear tests conducted with one direction of stress application as compared to those subjected to the multidirectional stress cycles representative of earthquake stresses in the field (Seed et al, 1975). These investigations have shown that the stresses required to cause liquefaction in uni-directional cyclic simple shear tests should be reduced

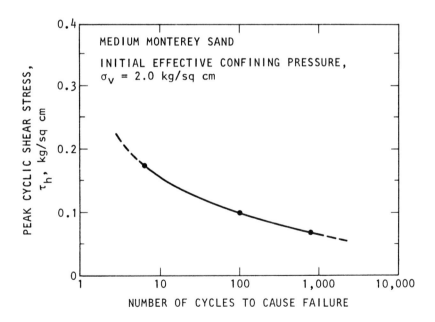

Figure 43. Typical form of the relationship between cyclic shear stress and the number of cycles to cause failure—simple shear conditions.

by about 10% to provide results representative of multidirectional shear conditions, and this correction factor is usually applied.

While the concepts involved in simple shear testing are simple, certain inherent difficulties in conducting the tests have long been recognized. These include:

1. Selection of representative samples
2. Avoidance of stress concentrations in the samples and the maintenance of uniform stresses and strains during the conduct of the test, and
3. Obtaining undisturbed samples of sand for the test program and maintaining a high level of undisturbance while the samples are set up in the test equipment.

While items 1 and 2 can be accomplished through the use of careful and skilled test techniques, it appears to be impossible to obtain undisturbed samples of most sands unless resort is made to the very expensive technique of freezing the soil prior to sampling. Accordingly, test data must be interpreted with a significant degree of judgment to allow for the possible effects of sample disturbance before being used for analysis purposes.

Cyclic Triaxial Compression Tests

Since equipment for conducting cyclic simple shear tests is not always available and because they offer improved possibilities for setting up undisturbed samples in the test equipment, cyclic load tests are often performed using triaxial compression test procedures. In the performance of these tests to represent level ground conditions in the field, samples are first consolidated under an ambient confining pressure, σ_a, and then subjected to cyclic deviator stress applications, σ_{dc}. Test data are similar in form to those obtained in cyclic simple shear tests and can be interpreted to determine the cyclic stress ratio, $\sigma_{dc}/2\sigma_a$, which causes liquefaction or cyclic mobility in the desired number of cycles.

Tests of this type do not represent field conditions nearly as well as do cyclic simple shear tests but it has been found that the cyclic stress ratio, τ_h / σ_v', causing liquefaction under multi-dimensional shaking conditions in the field is related to the cyclic stress ratio causing liquefaction of a triaxial test sample in the laboratory by the expression (Seed, 1979):

$$\left(\frac{\tau_h}{\sigma_v'}\right)_{\ell\text{-field}} \approx C_r \left(\frac{\sigma_{dc}}{2\sigma_a}\right)_{\ell\text{-triaxial}}$$

where values of C_r are approximately:

$$C_r = \begin{cases} 0.57 & \text{for } K_o = 0.4 \\ 0.9 \text{ to } 1 & \text{for } K_o = 1 \end{cases}$$

Experience indicates that carefully conducted cyclic triaxial tests performed and interpreted in this way can provide valid data on the cyclic loading characteristics of sands up to the development of pore pressure ratios of 100% and strains of the order of about 5% for dense samples or 20% for loose samples. Reliable data cannot be obtained, however, once necking of the sample occurs in any test specimen or if non-uniform conditions exist in the initial sample placement in the triaxial cell.

However, as in the case of cyclic simple shear tests, meaningful results can be obtained only if tests are performed on undisturbed samples representative of the in-situ deposit. Thus again, judgment is required to evaluate the possible effects of sample disturbance before using the test data for analysis purposes.

Effects of Sample Disturbance on Cyclic Loading Test Data

The cyclic loading characteristics of a natural sand deposit are strongly influenced by

1. Relative density of the deposit
2. Soil structure or grain arrangement, and
3. Cementation at grain contacts, which increases with the age of the deposit.

When a sampling tube is pushed into the sand, some disturbance inevitably occurs. For loose to medium dense sands, the movement of grains causes an increase in density (which tends to increase the cyclic loading resistance) but it also breaks down some of the cementation at grain contacts (which tends to reduce the cyclic loading resistance). The combined effect is apparently to cause little change in the cyclic loading resistance of the sand so that test data on good quality "undisturbed samples" give a good basis for evaluating the liquefaction potential of the deposit (Seed et al, 1982). This is illustrated by the successful use of data from undisturbed samples to predict, with an acceptable level of accuracy, the liquefaction of loose to medium dense sands at Lake Amatitlan (Seed et al, 1981), at Niigata (Ishihara and Koga, 1981) and at San Fernando (Seed et al, 1975).

For dense sands, however, the effects of sample disturbance are to cause dilation of the sand (which reduces the cyclic loading resistance) and to break down some of the cementation at grain contacts (which also reduces the cyclic loading resistance). As a result, the measured cyclic loading resistance of even good quality undisturbed samples is considerably less than that of the in-situ deposit and the liquefaction resistance appears to be much lower than is actually the case.

It should also be apparent from the above discussion that there is little hope of reconstituting the sand grains in the laboratory to the same density and structure they have in the field—a process which occurs in the field over a period of many years—and therefore it is necessary to attempt to obtain undisturbed samples for testing purposes. However, if this is not done by freezing, some judgment in the interpretation of test data from even good quality undisturbed samples will inevitably be required. In this respect, evaluations of liquefaction potential of sand deposits based on laboratory test data suffer from the same difficulty encountered in other design problems involving the properties of sands; that is, the key to obtaining acceptable evaluations of liquefaction or cyclic mobility potential depends primarily on the ability of the engineer to correctly evaluate the true in-situ properties of the soil involved from tests performed on samples that are inevitably disturbed in the sampling and handling process.

Applications of Cyclic Load Test Data for
Evaluating Soil Liquefaction Potential

The applicability of cyclic load test data for evaluating the liquefaction potential of soil deposits may be illustrated by a description of several case studies involving sands with different relative densities.

Case Study No. 1

Because of its familiarity, an interesting case study is the use of cyclic loading test data to evaluate the liquefaction potential of the sands in the light-damage and heavy-damage zones of Niigata, Japan. The elements of such a study were first presented in 1969 using estimated soil properties, but actual test data for the soils involved has recently been presented by Ishihari and Koga (1981). The average results of cyclic triaxial tests performed by these investigators on good quality undisturbed samples of sand taken in the depth range 10 to 25 ft. from two areas of Niigata, one where no liquefaction occurred in the 1964 earthquake and the area of Kawagishi-cho where extensive liquefaction occurred (see Fig. 3), are presented in Fig. 44. The soil profile in both areas consists of sand to substantial depths below the ground surface with the water table at a depth of about 4 ft.

The Niigata earthquake of 1964 had a Magnitude of about 7.5 and the source of energy release was about 50 km. from the city. From the curves presented in Fig. 20, the mean value of peak ground acceleration in Niigata would be estimated to be about 0.15g. It is of interest to note that a value of 0.16g was recorded at Kawagishi-cho and a slightly higher value (say as high as 0.18g) may well have developed in the non-liquefaction zones.

For the soil conditions in Niigata, the critical depth for liquefaction is about 20 ft. In accord with this fact and utilizing the data presented above, evaluations of liquefaction potential in the two different zones can be made as follows:

Area of Liquefaction (Kawagishi-cho)

Peak ground acceleration $\approx$ 0.16g

At depth of 20 ft:

$$\sigma_o \approx 20 \times 115 = 2300 \text{ psf}$$
$$\sigma_o' \approx 4 \times 115 + 16 \times 52.5 = 1300 \text{ psf}$$

Cyclic stress ratio developed by earthquake

$$\left(\frac{\tau_{av}}{\sigma_o'}\right)_d \approx 0.65 \cdot \frac{a_{max}}{g} \cdot \frac{\sigma_o}{\sigma_o'} \cdot r_d$$
$$\approx 0.65 \cdot 0.16 \cdot \frac{2300}{1300} \cdot 0.93 \approx 0.17$$

A Magnitude 7½ earthquake typically induces about 15 stress cycles but at Kawagishi-cho liquefaction occurred after about 3 significant cycles. From the data in Fig. 44, the cyclic stress

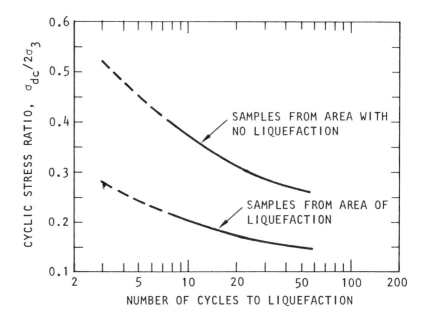

Figure 44. Results of cyclic loading triaxial tests on undisturbed samples, case study no. 1 (Data from Ishihare and Koga, 1981).

84

ratio causing liquefaction in 3 cycles is $\tau_{av}/\sigma_o' \approx 0.57 \times 0.28 \approx 0.16$. Since the induced stress ratio exceeds that causing liquefaction in 3 stress cycles, it can be concluded that the sand in the area is likely to liquefy early in the earthquake, as in fact it did.

Area of No Liquefaction

Peak ground acceleration ≈ 0.16 to $0.18g$

At depth of 20 ft.

$$\sigma_o \approx 20 \times 115 = 2300 \text{ psf}$$
$$\sigma_o' \approx 4 \times 115 + 16 \times 52.5 = 1300 \text{ psf}$$

Cyclic stress ratio developed by earthquake for $a_{max} = 0.18g$

$$\left(\frac{\tau_{av}}{\sigma_o'}\right)_d \approx 0.65 \cdot 0.18 \cdot \frac{2300}{1300} \cdot 0.93 \approx 0.19$$

A Magnitude 7.5 earthquake produces 15 equivalent uniform stress cycles. The cyclic stress ratio causing liquefaction in 15 cycles is

$$\left(\frac{\tau_{av}}{\sigma_o'}\right)_\ell \approx 0.57 \times 0.34 \approx 0.195$$

based on the data in Fig. 44. Thus the soil in this zone would have a small margin of safety against liquefaction at a depth of 20 ft. It may be noted that if a soil does not quite liquefy it remains stable. However, the observed stability is not necessarily indicative of the closeness of catastrophic failure.

It may be seen that in this case-study, the use of ground motion attenuation curves, simple theory and laboratory test data on undisturbed samples taken in thin-wall tubes could have correctly predicted the soil behavior in the Niigata area. Similar results seem to apply to other medium dense sand deposits.

Case Study No. 2

In the process of developing a site, undesirable soils were excavated and replaced by a densely compacted sand fill having

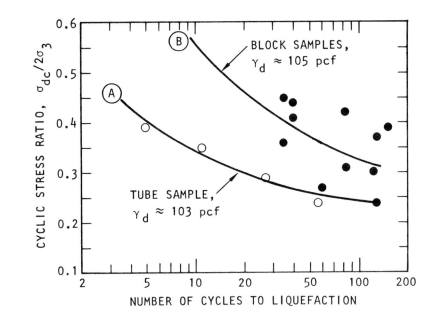

Figure 45. Results of cyclic loading triaxial tests on undisturbed samples, case study no. 2 (Data from Marcuson and Franklin, 1979).

a dry density of 113 pcf. After placement, the water table stabilized at a depth of 10 ft. below the ground surface. Because the site was located in a seismically active region, it was considered desirable to evaluate the liquefaction potential of the sand for a maximum ground acceleration of 0.25g produced by a Magnitude 7.5 earthquake. For this purpose, good-quality "undisturbed" samples were taken in thin-wall sampling tubes and subjected to cyclic triaxial tests to evaluate the liquefaction characteristics of the sand. The results of these tests are shown by curve A in Fig. 45. On the basis of these results the liquefaction potential was determined as follows:

For a critical depth of about 20 ft:

$$\sigma_o \approx 20 \times 120 = 2400 \text{ psf}$$

$$\sigma_o' \approx 10 \times 120 + 10 \times 60 = 1800 \text{ psf}$$

The cyclic stress ratio developed by the earthquake

$$\left(\frac{\tau_{av}}{\sigma_o{}'}\right)_d \approx 0.65 \cdot \frac{a_{max}}{g} \cdot \frac{\sigma_o}{\sigma_o{}'} \cdot r_d$$

$$\approx 0.65 \cdot 0.25 \cdot \frac{2400}{1800} \cdot 0.93 \approx 0.2$$

A Magnitude 7.5 earthquake causes approximately 15 equivalent stress cycles. From the data on curve A in Fig. 45, the cyclic stress ratio causing liquefaction in 15 cycles is

$$\left(\frac{\tau_{av}}{\sigma_o{}'}\right)_\ell \approx 0.57 \times 0.32 \approx 0.18$$

Since the stress ratio developed exceeds this value, it appears that the sand would liquefy in the design earthquake.

To explore this further, a second set of undisturbed samples were taken by block sampling from a test pit. The cyclic load test data for specimens trimmed from the block samples are shown by Curve B in Fig. 45. For these results, the cyclic stress ratio required to cause liquefaction of the sand in 15 cycles is found to be

$$\left(\frac{\tau_{av}}{\sigma_o{}'}\right)_\ell \approx 0.57 \times 0.5 \approx 0.28$$

and the factor of safety against liquefaction is

$$\frac{\left(\frac{\tau_{av}}{\sigma_o{}'}\right)_\ell}{\left(\frac{\tau_{av}}{\sigma_o{}'}\right)_d} \approx \frac{0.28}{0.20} \approx 1.4$$

On further investigation it was found that the average dry density of the compacted fill was about 112 pcf, the average dry density of the block samples was 105 pcf, and the average dry density of the thin-wall tube samples was 103 pcf. Because of its higher density, the fill actually has a factor of safety greater than that indicated by the tests on block samples and much greater than that indicated by the tests on thin-wall "undisturbed" tube samples.

This case* illustrates the significant effects of disturbance, resulting from dilation and loosening of the soil in the sampling process, when undisturbed samples of dense sand are taken by pushing sampling tubes into the deposit. As a result the test data does not reflect the true cyclic loading resistance of the sand and grossly misleading results may be obtained unless good judgment is used in the test data interpretation.

Evaluation of Liquefaction Potential of Sand Deposits Based on Observations in Previous Earthquakes

An alternative procedure to the use of laboratory tests as a means of evaluating the resistance to liquefaction of sand deposits is to correlate known values of the cyclic stress ratio exhibited by sands under actual earthquake shaking conditions with some readily measurable in-situ characteristics of the sands. By this means any questions about the accuracy with which laboratory tests simulate field loading conditions or about the effects of sample disturbance on the test results are circumvented. In effect, real earthquakes are used to perform "ideal" tests and the results are correlated with a convenient index of soil properties.

Japanese engineers were the first to use this procedure in adopting the standard penetration resistance of the Niigata sand as a means of differentiating between liquefiable and non-liquefiable conditions in the Niigata earthquake. The procedure has been progressively refined since that time and it now provides a reliable basis for evaluating the liquefaction potential (Seed and Idriss, 1982).

The essential features of this approach are: (1) to develop some basic framework on which to organize past field experiences of liquefaction and non-liquefaction; and (2) to determine a suitable index of soil liquefaction characteristics which is easily determined and which can reasonably be correlated with soil liquefaction characteristics. These two components of the approach are discussed separately below.

*It should be noted that this case is semi-hypothetical in that the design problem has been changed from the actual conditions. However, the test data were obtained in an actual investigation of the properties of a test fill conducted by the U.S. Army Corps of Engineers (Marcuson and Franklin, 1979).

Use of Field Data to Evaluate Cyclic Loading Characteristics

In interpreting the results of laboratory cyclic loading tests, it soon became apparent that a convenient parameter for expressing the cyclic liquefaction characteristics of a sand under level ground conditions is the cyclic stress ratio; that is, the ratio of the average cyclic shear stress, τ_h, developed on horizontal surfaces during cyclic loading to the initial vertical effective stress, $\sigma_o{}'$, acting on the sand before the cyclic stresses were applied. This parameter has the advantage of taking into account the intensity of the earthquake shaking or other cyclic loading phenomena which determine τ_h and the initial effective stresses on the soil which determine liquefiability and reflect the influence of the depth of a soil element in the ground and the depth of the water table at a site.

In determining analytically the shear stresses induced by an earthquake on horizontal surfaces of a deposit, it was also found that the average shear stress τ_h can be expressed approximately by the equation (see Eq. 4):

$$\tau_h \approx 0.65 \cdot \frac{a_{max}}{g} \cdot \sigma_c \cdot r_d$$

Thus the stress ratio developed on a soil element in the field during an earthquake can be expressed by

$$\frac{\tau_h}{\sigma_o{}'} \approx 0.65 \cdot \frac{a_{max}}{g} \cdot \frac{\sigma_o}{\sigma_o{}'} \cdot r_d$$

and this stress ratio can readily be computed for any soil element in any earthquake, provided the appropriate values of a_{max}, σ_o, σ_o' and r_d can be evaluated. For soil elements at depths less than about 40 ft, values of σ_o, σ_o' and r_d can be estimated with a high degree of accuracy from a knowledge of the soil profile and the general soil conditions. Thus, values of the cyclic stress ratio induced in the ground by an earthquake can readily be determined provided the maximum ground surface acceleration is known.

With increasing use of strong motion recording instruments in seismically active regions, increasing numbers of sand deposits are being subjected to field loading by earthquakes in which good records of maximum ground accelerations are obtained. In these events, it can be determined whether the sand liquefies or does not liquefy under the levels of stress ratio developed. Thus each such case study provides a field test data point reflecting whether liquefaction did or did not occur under a given level of applied cyclic stress ratio. When a significant number of such data points are determined, they provide a means for determining boundary values separating liquefaction-producing from non-liquefaction-producing conditions, solely on the basis of field case studies.

This type of approach is always appealing to engineers and it can readily be applied provided that the field results are correlated with some index of soil properties which enables the liquefaction characteristics of sands at different sites to be compared with each other on a reliable basis. Index tests suitable for this purpose are discussed below.

Index Tests for Soil Liquefaction Characteristics

The first reasonably comprehensive collection of site conditions where evidence indicating that either liquefaction or no liquefaction had taken place was presented in 1971 by Seed and Peacock, and used as a basis to determine the relationship between field values of cyclic stress ratio causing liquefaction and the relative density of the sands, as determined by the Standard Penetration Resistance and its correlation with relative density proposed by Gibbs and Holtz (1957). This collection of field cases is shown in Fig. 46. With increased understanding of the factors influencing the liquefaction characteristics of sands, however, it soon became clear that factors other than the relative density of a sand had a significant influence on cyclic loading soil behavior. These factors included:

1. Relative density
2. Soil structure or fabric
3. Aging, or the development of cementation at grain contacts with increasing time under pressure
4. Lateral earth pressure coefficient, K_o
5. Seismic history of the deposit.

90

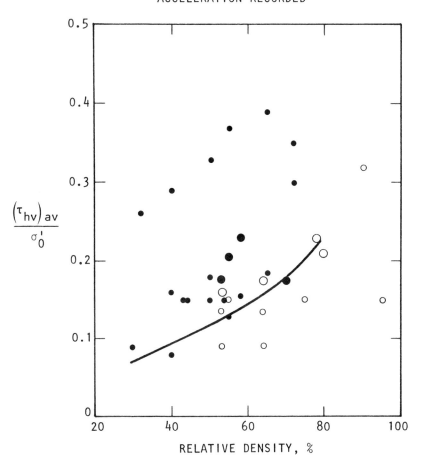

Figure 46. Relationship between average cyclic stress ratio and relative density for known cases of liquefaction and non-liquefaction.

91

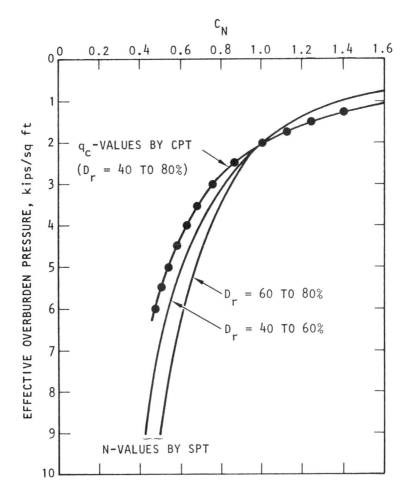

Figure 47. Chart for values of C_N.

Interestingly, all of these factors affect the cyclic loading characteristics of sands and the penetration resistance in the same general way. Changes in the factors that tend to increase the cyclic loading resistance also tend to increase the penetration resistance. Thus it is more meaningful to use penetration resistance directly as an index of liquefaction resistance than to use an individual factor such as relative density. More recent correlations of field data have recognized this fact and used penetration resistance directly rather than some other property. It would seem to make little difference whether the test used were the Standard Penetration Test (SPT) or the Cone Penetration Test (CPT) since either is likely to be a good indicator of cyclic loading liquefaction characteristics. However, because of its widespread use in areas where earthquakes have occurred, the Standard Penetration Test has provided virtually all the field test data available for field liquefaction studies.

Since the standard penetration resistance, N, measured in the field actually reflects the influence of the soil properties and the effective confining pressure, it has been found desirable to eliminate the influence of confining pressure by using a normalized penetration resistance N_1, where N_1 is the measured penetration of the soil under an effective overburden pressure of 1 ton per sq. ft. The value of N_1 for any sand can be determined from the measured value N from the relationship

$$N_1 = C_N \cdot N$$

where C_N is a function of the effective overburden pressure at the depth where the penetration test was conducted. Values of C_N may be read off from the chart shown in Fig. 47, which is based on studies conducted at the Waterways Experiment Station (Bieganousky and Marcuson, 1976; Marcuson and Bieganousky, 1977).

In principle there is no reason why other index characteristics (such as possible electrical properties, shear wave velocity or other in-situ test data) can not be correlated with cyclic loading characteristics determined in the field. However, there is very little field test data available to establish good correlations of field performance with any soil characteristics other than the standard penetration resistance at the present time. This situation will no doubt change with time as other index properties are determined for soils whose liquefaction resistance has been established by earthquake shaking and possibly improved correlations will be developed. Furthermore, other parameters can potentially be measured more accurately, over a wider depth range and in more difficult environmental conditions than can the standard penetration resistance. At the present time, however, no such choice exists.

The Standard Penetration Test

Various studies in recent years have shown the potential variability in the conditions utilized in this supposedly standardized test procedure which was intended to measure the number of blows (of a 140 lb hammer falling freely through a height of 30 inches) required to drive a standard sampling tube (2″ O.D. and 1½″ I.D.) 12 inches into the ground. For example, Kovacs et al (1977, 1978) made careful investigations of the energy in the hammer at its impact with the top of the sampling rod-anvil system, when using the conventional practice of lifting the hammer by means of a rope wrapped around a rotating drum, as compared with an ideal triggering device giving a truly free fall to the 140-lb. drive weight. It was found that typically the energy in the hammer at impact when using the rope and drum procedure with two turns of the rope was only about 60% of that delivered by a free-falling weight. For three turns this was reduced to 40%; other minor variations were introduced by using old or new rope and changing the speed of the pulley. The authors concluded that an energy standard should be adopted as a criterion for the SPT test and in the meantime, all pertinent test conditions should be made a standard part of the boring log to aid in interpreting the results.

From recent comprehensive theoretical and field studies of the standard penetration test at the University of Florida, Palacios (1977) and Schmertmann (1976, 1977) concluded that the results may be significantly influenced by such factors as: (1) The use of drilling mud versus casing for supporting the walls of the drill hole; (2) the use of a hollow stem augur versus casing and water; (3) the size of the drill hole; (4) the number of turns of the rope around the drum; (5) the use of a small or large anvil; (6) the length of the drive rods; (7) the use of nonstandard sampling tubes; and (8) the depth range (0 to 12 in. or 6 in. to 18 in.) over which the penetration resistance is measured.

Both Schmertmann and Kovacs et al concluded that a necessary prerequisite to the satisfactory use of the standard penetration test as a measure of any soil characteristic is an increased degree of standardization. Schmertmann (1977) suggests that this is particularly true with respect to: the amount of energy delivered into the drilling rods, and the use of rotary drilling methods and a drill hole continuously filled with drilling mud.

If this approach is adopted, much of the variability can be eliminated by adopting standard test conditions and applying corrections for others. Thus in the present report, the loss of driving energy which results from using a short length of rods is corrected by multiplying the measured N values in the depth range 0 to 10 ft. by a factor of 0.75, and other aspects of the test are standardized by using data from tests performed under the following conditions:

1. The use of a rope and drum system, with two turns of the rope around the drum, to lift the falling weight

2. Drilling mud to support the sides of the hole

3. A relatively small diameter hole, approximately 4 inches in diameter, and

4. Penetration resistance measured over the range 6 to 18 inches penetration into the ground.

While it is recognized that these conditions do not represent the standard prescribed in the ideal test procedure, they represent conditions widely used for many years both in North America and in other countries throughout the world, and they have been used in establishing much of the field data available for liquefaction correlations. Thus their adoption for this monograph is justified for this reason alone. Where test conditions deviate from those listed above, appropriate corrections to the measured results should be made before using the correlation charts presented herein.

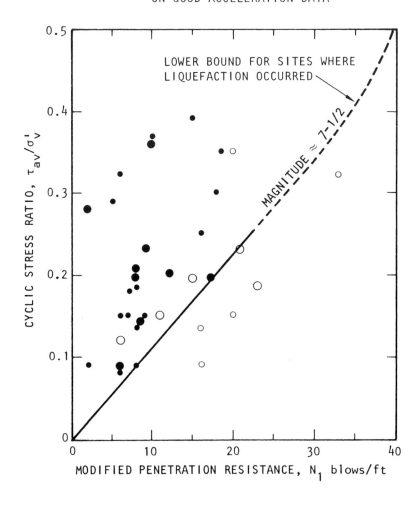

● LIQUEFACTION: STRESS RATIO BASED ON ESTIMATED ACCELERATION
● LIQUEFACTION: STRESS RATIO BASED ON GOOD ACCELERATION DATA
○ NO LIQUEFACTION: STRESS RATIO BASED ON ESTIMATED ACCELERATION
○ NO LIQUEFACTION: STRESS RATIO BASED ON GOOD ACCELERATION DATA

Figure 48. Correlation between stress ratio causing liquefaction in the field and penetration resistance of sand.

96

Method of Interpreting Field Data and Evaluating
Liquefaction Potential

The use of field data in developing a relationship between cyclic stress ratio causing liquefaction and standard penetration resistance may be illustrated by analysis of the results presented in Fig. 35. The data show, for example, that for the conditions in Niigata, a standard penetration resistance value of about 14 blows/foot at a depth of 20 ft. is representative of a marginal liquefaction condition.

Considering that the maximum ground acceleration in the general area of Niigata was probably about 0.18g in this earthquake (Magnitude $\approx$ 7.5) and that the water table was about 4 ft. below the ground surface, the following results may be determined for a depth of 20 ft.:

Total overburden pressure, $\sigma_o \approx 20 \times 115 = 2300\,\text{psf}$

Effective overburden pressure, $\sigma_o' \approx 4 \times 115 + 16 \times 52.5$
$$= 1300\,\text{psf}$$

For $\sigma_o' = 1300\,\text{psf}$, $C_N = 1.2$ and $N_1 = 1.2 \times 14 \approx 17$

At depth of 20 ft., $r_d \approx 0.93$ (from Fig. 40)

Thus $\dfrac{T_h}{\sigma_o'} \approx 0.65 \cdot \dfrac{a_{max}}{g} \cdot \dfrac{\sigma_o}{\sigma_o'} \cdot r_d$

$$\approx 0.65 \cdot 0.18 \cdot \frac{2300}{1300} \cdot 0.93$$

$$\approx 0.19$$

It may be concluded therefore that for a Magnitude 7.5 earthquake, a sand having an N_1 value of 17 was found to just liquefy under an induced average cyclic stress ratio of 0.19. A point indicating this conclusion can therefore be plotted on the diagram shown in Fig. 48.

By collecting data from a number of sites where the maximum ground surface accelerations are known and where the behavior of the soil is known (liquefied or not liquefied), a number of points representing the different conditions can be plotted in Fig. 48 and a boundary can be drawn separating conditions known to cause liquefaction from those where liquefaction did not occur. In Fig. 48 the boundary line shown is meant to be a lower bound for such a line and the boundary is representative of Magnitude 7.5 earthquakes. The data shown in this figure represent the field data base available in 1975.

With the aid of a plot such as that shown in Fig. 48 it is a simple matter to evaluate the liquefaction or cyclic mobility potential of any other site. For the given site and the design earthquake for which it must be evaluated, it is simply necessary to determine the values of N_1 for the sand layers involved, read off from Fig. 48 the lower bound values of τ_{av}/σ_o' for sites where some evidence of liquefaction is known to have occurred for soils with those N_1 values, and compare these stress ratios with those induced by the design earthquake for the site under investigation. This procedure has been widely used to evaluate the liquefaction potential of soil deposits, and it is recommended in the Tentative Provisions for the Development of Seismic Regulations for Buildings (Applied Technology Council, 1978).

Recent Field Data

One of the greatest limitations of the plot shown in Fig. 48 at the time it was first presented was the limited number of reliable data points available to define the boundary separating liquefiable from non-liquefiable sites. A second limitation was its inability to differentiate between appropriate boundaries for different magnitude earthquakes.

In the past six years, however, supplementary data has been provided from a variety of sources to greatly increase the data base. Sources of this data include the following:

Data from Chinese Building Code (1974)

Liquefaction studies in mainland China, conducted independently but along similar lines to those developed in the United States, have also led to a correlation between earthquake shaking conditions causing liquefaction or cyclic mobility and the standard penetration resistance of sands (Ref. 9). In this correlation, the critical value of the standard penetration resistance, N_{crit}, separating liquefiable from non-liquefiable conditions to a depth of approximately 50 ft. is determined by

$$N_{crit} = \overline{N}[1 + 0.125 (d_s - 3) - 0.05 (d_w - 2)]$$

in which d_s = depth to sand layer under consideration in meters; d_w = depth of water below ground surface in meters; and $\overline{N}$ = a function of the shaking intensity as follows:

Modified Mercalli Intensity	$\overline{N}$ in blows per foot
VII	6
VIII	10
IX	16

This correlation, for a water table depth of 2 m, reduced to the same parameters as those used in Fig. 48 with the aid of the correlation between earthquake shaking intensity and maximum ground acceleration developed by Trifunac and Brady (1976), is plotted in Fig. 49, where it is also compared with the lower bound line for sites showing evidence of some degree of cyclic mobility or liquefaction shown in Fig. 48. It may be seen that there is a high degree of agreement between the critical boundary determined in this way and that shown in Fig. 48. It is significant and remarkable that such a great similarity in both procedures and criteria should have evolved in countries with so little technical communication at the time that the individual plots were developed.

Data from the Haicheng and Tangshan Earthquakes in China (1974, 1976)

More recent data for 9 sites known to have liquefied and 5 for which there was no apparent liquefaction in the Haicheng (1974) and Tangshan (1976) earthquakes in China (Magnitudes 7.3 and 7.8 respectively) have been presented by Xie (1979). These data, reduced to the form shown in Fig. 48 with the aid

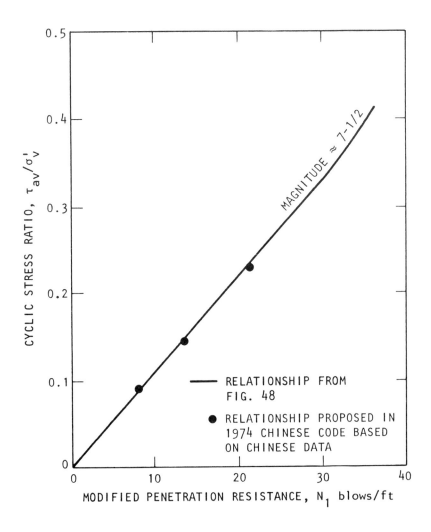

Figure 49. Comparison of empirical chart for predicting liquefaction with recommendations of 1974 Chinese code.

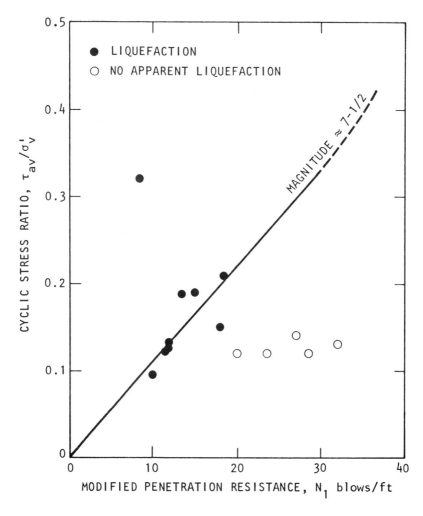

Figure 50. Comparison of empirical chart for predicting liquefaction with data from Haicheng and Tangshan earthquakes.

of the Trifunac and Brady correlation between intensity and peak ground acceleration, are shown in Fig. 50 together with the boundary line from Fig. 48.

Data from the Guatemala Earthquake (1976)

During the Guatemala earthquake of 1976 (Magnitude 7.6) extensive liquefaction occurred in the area of La Playa on the edge of Lake Amatitlan. A detailed report of field and laboratory studies of the soil conditions in the area affected, in the adjacent area where no liquefaction occurred, and just beyond the boundary of the liquefied zone has been presented by Seed et al (1981). The correlation between induced stress ratio τ_{av} / σ_o' and the normalized SPT values for the different zones is shown in Fig. 51, where they are again compared with the boundary line separating sites known to have liquefied or not liquefied, taken from Fig. 48.

Data from the Argentina Earthquake (1977)

In November, 1977 a major earthquake with Magnitude $\approx$ 7.4 occurred in San Juan Province, Argentina, and relationships between induced stress ratio determined from ground acceleration and standard penetration test data for 11 sites where liquefaction occurred and 9 sites where liquefaction did not occur have been presented by Idriss et al (1979). Penetration data for the liquefied sites were taken in adjacent areas where liquefaction was not apparent. The results of these studies are presented in Fig. 52.

Data from Miyagiken-Oki Earthquake, Japan (1978)

An abundant series of new data points, obtained primarily as a result of studies following the Miyagiken-Oki earthquake in Japan in June, 1978 (Magnitude $\approx$ 7.4) were presented by Tokimatsu and Yoshimi (1981). The data were originally presented in a slightly different form from that used in the plots shown in Figs. 48 to 52, but they can readily be converted to the same form on the basis of the information provided in the report.

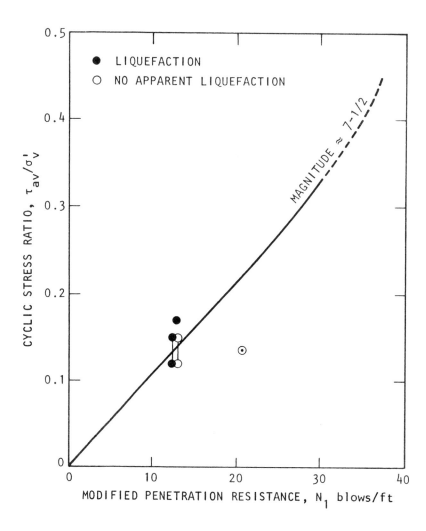

Figure 51. Comparison of empirical chart for predicting liquefaction with data from Guatemala earthquake, 1976.

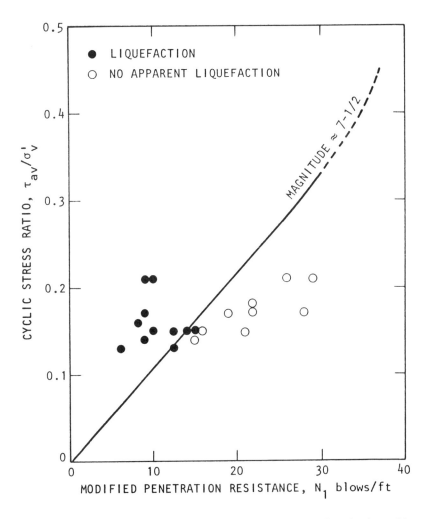

Figure 52. Comparison of empirical chart for predicting liquefaction with data from Argentina earthquake, 1977.

For sands with a mean grain diameter $D_{50} > 0.25$ mm, the corrected data from this study are shown in Fig. 53 where they are compared with the boundary line determined in Fig. 48. It may be seen that there is generally good agreement although some sites where liquefaction apparently did not occur are found to plot above the boundary line. It is appropriate that this may occur since sites where liquefaction is not reported can not be considered with the same degree of confidence as sites where evidence of liquefaction is clearly apparent. This is due to the fact that in the absence of surface evidence of liquefaction, a site can only be classified as one with "no apparent liquefaction" since there is some possibility that liquefaction may have occurred at some depth below the ground surface but its effects were not evidenced at the ground surface. Viewed in this light, the data points shown in Fig. 53 may be considered good confirmatory evidence of the position of the boundary line shown for sandy sites and Magnitude $\approx 7\frac{1}{2}$ earthquakes.

Summary of Field Data for Sands

The reliable field data from Fig. 48 together with the supplementary data shown in Figs. 49 to 53 are plotted together in Fig. 54 where they provide a significantly greater data base from which to determine a boundary line (or zone) separating sites known to have liquefied from sites which have apparently not liquefied in a series of earthquakes, all of which have magnitudes of about $7\frac{1}{2}$. The data for Niigata and Lake Amatitlan are known to be at the boundary for such a line, and the Chinese code results are also intended to define limiting conditions. Thus a revised position for the boundary line for sands can now be established. Fortunately this boundary is very close to that shown in Fig. 48 but it is supported by a significantly greater data base and thus can be drawn with a far greater degree of confidence than heretofore.

Field Data for Silty Sands

The study of sites in the Miyagiken-Oki earthquake by Tokimatsu and Yoshimi (1981) also presented an extensive set of field data points for silty sands ($D_{50} < 0.15$ mm). Japanese

105

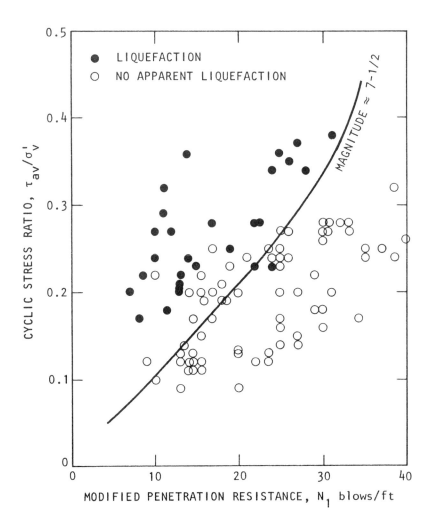

Figure 53. Correlation between field liquefaction behavior of sands (D_{50} > 0.25 mm) under level ground conditions and standard penetration resistance in Miyagiken-Oki earthquake, 1978 (Data after Tokimatsu and Yoshimi).

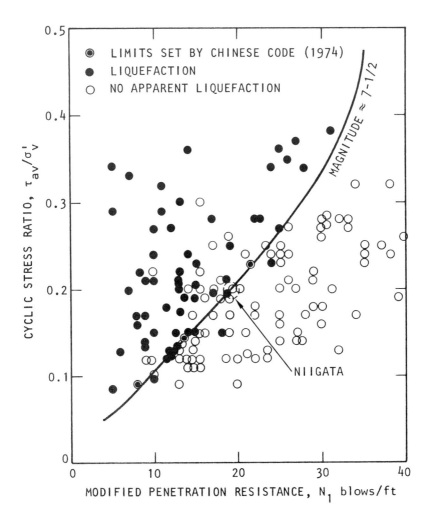

Figure 54. Corection between field liquefaction behavior of sands ($D_{50} > 0.25$ mm) under level ground conditions and standard penetration resistance (all data)—effective overburden pressures less than 1 TSF.

engineers (e.g. Tatsuoka, Iwasaki et al, 1980) have considered for the past several years, on the basis of laboratory test data, that silty sands are considerably less vulnerable to liquefaction than sands with similar penetration resistance values and the site studies provided by Tokimatsu and Yoshimi provide good field corroboration that this is in fact the case. The data for silty sands, for sites which liquefied and sites with no apparent liquefaction, are presented in Fig. 55 in the same form as the data in Fig. 54. Also shown in the figure are a reasonable boundary separating sites where liquefaction occurred and sites where no liquefaction occurred for these silty sand deposits, and the boundary line for sands taken from Fig. 54. It may be seen that the boundary line for silty sands is significantly higher than the boundary line for sandy soils, although the two lines are essentially parallel. In fact for any value of stress ratio, the normalized standard penetration resistance, N_1, for sands with $D_{50} > 0.25$ mm is essentially equal to that for silty sands ($D_{50} < 0.15$ mm) plus 7.5. It may be concluded therefore that the boundary previously established for sands can be used for silty sands, provided the N_1 value for the silty sand site is increased by 7.5 before entering the chart. This correction can have a very significant effect on liquefaction evaluations for silty sand deposits.

It is interesting to note that Zhou (1981) reached a similar conclusion on the basis of field studies in China following the Tangshan earthquake. From a comparison of the behavior of different types of soil, Zhou concluded that correlations between penetration resistance (in this case, static cone penetration resistance) and liquefaction characteristics for sands are not applicable for silty sands unless they are modified to allow for the fines content of the silty sands. Zhou proposed that for soils with the same penetration resistance, this allowance might take the form of an increase in penetration resistance, the magnitude depending on the fines content. For soils with about 30% fines (which would correspond approximately to soils with $D_{50} < 0.15$ mm), the desirable increase in static cone resistance was found to be about 27 kg/cm^2, which corresponds, for the site conditions involved, to an increase in N_1 value of about 6. This is in remarkably good agreement with the value of 7.5 indicated by the results presented previously.

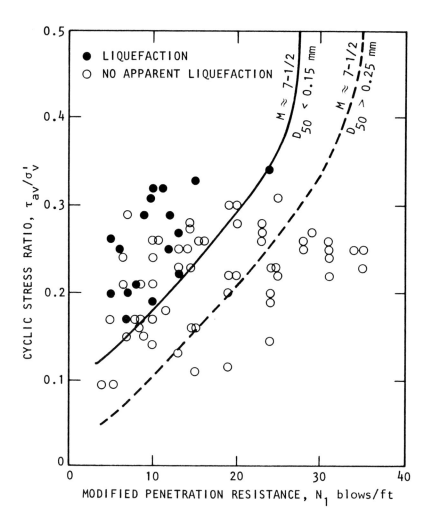

Figure 55. Correlation between field liquefaction behavior of silty sands (D_{50} < 0.15 mm) under level ground conditions and standard penetration resistance (Data after Tokimatsu and Yoshimi, 1981).

109

Correlations for Different Magnitude Earthquakes

The preceding results provide a realistic basis for developing correlations between standard penetration tests and the liquefaction characteristics of sands and silty sands for Magnitude $\approx$ 7½ earthquakes. These results can be extended to other magnitude events by noting that from a liquefaction point of view, the main difference between different magnitude events is in the number of cycles of stress which they induce. Statistical studies (Seed et al, 1975) show that the number of cycles representative of different magnitude earthquakes is typically as shown in the following table:

Earthquake Magnitude, M	No. of representative cycles at $0.65\,\tau_{max}$
8½	26
7½	15
6¾	10
6	5–6
5¼	2–3

A representative shape for the relationship between cyclic stress ratio and number of cycles required to cause liquefaction is shown in Fig. 56. If the number of cycles, 15, for a magnitude 7½ event is used as a basis for comparison, then the relative values of stress ratio required to cause liquefaction for other numbers of cycles may be expressed as ratios of the ordinates of the curve in Fig. 56 relative to the ordinates corresponding to 15 cycles. These ratios are shown directly on the plot and summarized below:

Earthquake Magnitude, M	No. of representative cycles at $0.65\,\tau_{max}$	$\dfrac{\left(\dfrac{\tau_{av}}{\sigma_o{}'}\right)_{\ell-M\,=\,M}}{\left(\dfrac{\tau_{av}}{\sigma_o{}'}\right)_{\ell-M\,=\,7.5}}$
8½	26	0.89
7½	15	1.0
6¾	10	1.13
6	5–6	1.32
5¼	2–3	1.5

110

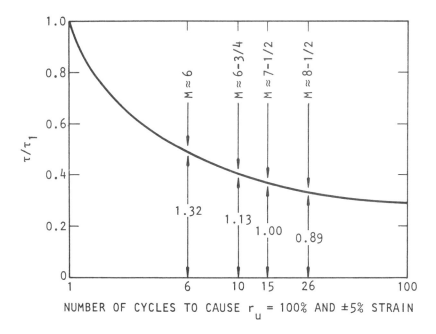

Figure 56. Representative relationship between τ/τ_1 and number of cycles required to cause liquefaction.

Thus by multiplying the boundary curve in Fig. 54 by the scaling factors shown in column 3 of the above table, boundary curves separating sites where liquefaction is likely to occur or unlikely to occur may be determined for earthquakes with different magnitudes. Such a family of curves for sands is shown in Fig. 57. The same curves may be used for silty sands provided the normalized standard penetration resistance, N_1, for the silty sand is increased by 7.5 before entering the chart.

Liquefaction of Clayey Soils

Both laboratory tests and field performance data have shown that the great majority of clayey soils will not liquefy during earthquakes. However, recent studies in China (Wang, 1979) have shown that certain types of clayey materials may be vulnerable to severe strength loss as a result of earthquake shaking. These soils appear to have the following characteristics:

111

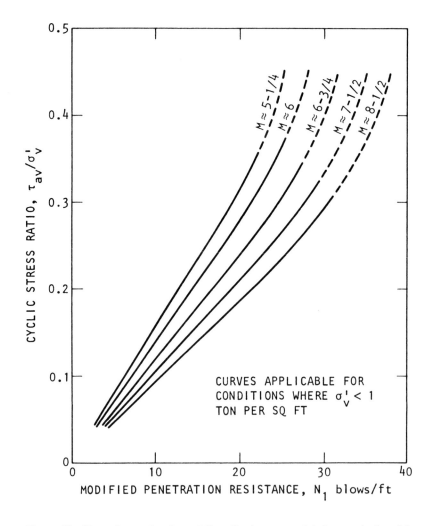

Figure 57. Chart for evaluation of liquefaction potential for sands for different magnitude earthquakes.

Percent finer than 0.005 mm $< 15\%$
Liquid Limit < 35
Water Content $> 0.9 \times$ Liquid Limit

If soils with these characteristics plot above the A-line on the Plasticity chart, the best means of determining their cyclic loading characteristics is by test. Otherwise, clayey soils may be considered non-vulnerable to liquefaction.

Determination of Pore Pressure Increase in Sandy or Silty Soils

In some cases it may be desirable to evaluate the potential pore pressure increase due to a given intensity of earthquake shaking in sandy soils. A simple approximate means for accomplishing this is to use the normalized form of pore pressure increase curves proposed by Lee and Albeisa (1974) and DeAlba et al (1976), shown in Fig. 58. Experience indicates that for many sands under level ground conditions, the relationship between induced pore pressure ratio, u_g/σ_o', and cycle ratio N_e/N_l where N_e is the number of equivalent cycles induced by the earthquake and N_l is the number of such cycles required to cause liquefaction, will lie between the boundaries shown in

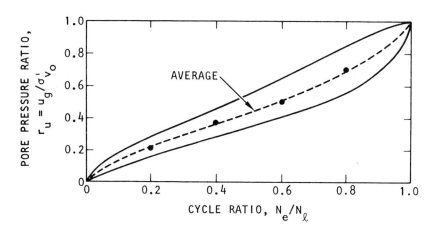

Figure 58. Rate of pore water pressure buildup in cyclic simple shear tests (After DeAlba et al., 1975).

113

Fig. 58. Thus if for any given site and any given earthquake magnitude, the factor of safety against liquefaction is determined by the correlation charts to be greater than 1, then the induced pore pressure may be estimated as follows:

1. Determine the average cyclic stress ratio induced by the earthquake and the factor of safety against liquefaction.

2. Determine the number of effective stress cycles (at $0.65\tau_{max}$) induced by the earthquake (N_e).

3. Plot the induced effects (induced stress ratio expressed as the ordinate of the curve shown in Fig. 56 divided by the factor of safety) versus the number of cycles as a point on Fig. 56.

4. For the ordinate of the point determined in step 3 above, read off from the curve the number of cycles required to cause liquefaction, N_ℓ.

5. Hence, determine the Cycle Ratio $= N_e/N_\ell$.

6. For the determined value of Cycle Ratio, read off the induced pore pressure ratio, $u_g/\sigma_o{}'$, from Fig. 58.

In a recent study, Ishihara (1981) measured the pore pressure buildup in a sand deposit in Tokyo Bay resulting from a Magnitude 6 earthquake producing a maximum ground surface acceleration at the site of 0.1g. The normalized SPT value, N_1, for the silty sand in which pore pressures were measured was 10, and the pore pressure ratio induced by the earthquake was about 0.15. The pore pressures induced in the deposit, computed by the procedure described above, lie in the range 0.07 to 0.15, indicating that the method provides useful results for cases of partial pore pressure buildup.

Use of SPT Correlation Charts with CPT Data

While the Standard Penetration Test (SPT) has been widely used for many years, in many cases it may be more expedient to explore the variability of conditions within an extensive sand deposit using the static cone penetration test (CPT). In this test a cone with a diameter of about 1.4 inches is pushed into the ground and the resistance to penetration of the conical tip, q_c, is measured in units of kg/cm^2.

The main advantages of this procedure are that it provides data much more rapidly than does the SPT test, it provides a continuous record of penetration resistance in any bore hole, and it is less vulnerable to operator error than the SPT test.

The main disadvantage of the test, from the point of view of predicting the liquefaction resistance of a site, is that it has a very limited data base to provide a correlation between soil liquefaction characteristics and CPT values. This data base may remain meager for some time pending the generation of new data from new earthquakes. In the meantime, CPT data can be used in conjunction with the extensive data base for the Standard Penetration Test by either:

1. Conducting preliminary studies at each new site to establish a correlation between CPT data and N values for the sand at the site (see, for example, the study by Douglas et al, 1981), or

2. Using available correlations between SPT test data and CPT test data based on test programs previously conducted. Thus the average relationships between q_c determined from CPT data and N values in SPT tests are approximately (Schmertmann, 1978):

$$q_c = \begin{cases} 4 \text{ to } 5 \text{ N} & \text{for clean sands} \\ 3.5 \text{ to } 4.5 \text{ N} & \text{for silty sands} \end{cases}$$

With such relationships, the data obtained from CPT test programs can readily be converted to equivalent N values for the sand and then used in conjunction with the charts in Figs. 54 to 57 to evaluate liquefaction resistance. By this means, full advantage can be taken of the merits of the CPT test procedure and the extensive data base of the SPT correlation with field liquefaction characteristics.

Alternatively, the critical boundaries separating liquefiable from non-liquefiable conditions shown in Figs. 54, 55 and 57 can be expressed in terms of a static cone penetration resistance corresponding to an overburden pressure of 1 ton per sq. ft., q_{c_1}, by using the relationships

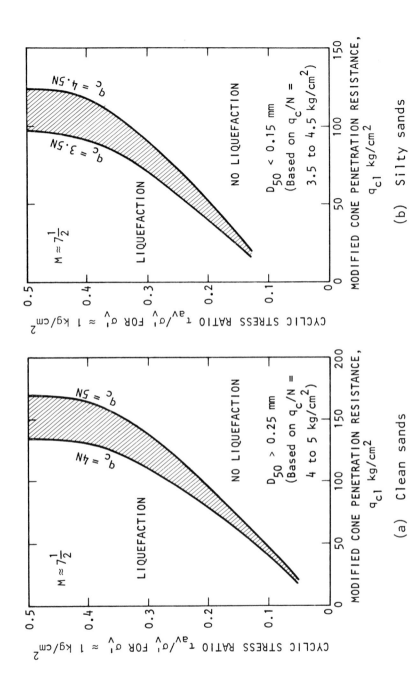

Figure 59. Correlation between field liquefaction behavior of sands under level ground conditions and static cone penetration resistance.

$$q_{c_1} \approx \begin{cases} 4 \text{ to } 5 \text{ N}_1 \text{ for clean sands} \\ 3.5 \text{ to } 4.5 \text{ N}_1 \text{ for silty sands} \end{cases}$$

This would lead to plots relating values of cyclic stress ratio causing liquefaction with q_{c_1} values as shown in Fig. 59.

It is interesting to note that for any sand the value of q_{c_1} can be determined from the value of q_c measured at any depth using the relationship

$$q_{c_1} = q_c \cdot C_N$$

where values of C_N are read off from the curve shown in Fig. 47 which is based on the relationship between q_c, effective overburden pressure and relative density proposed by Schmertmann (1978).

In view of the need to introduce a second correlation (between SPT and CPT), this procedure would seem to be less desirable than use of the SPT directly as an index of liquefaction. However, in view of the other advantages of the cone penetration test (more continuous and extensive records of soil characteristics) and the fact that site-specific correlations can be developed where appropriate, this procedure may well prove advantageous in many cases.

Conclusions Regarding the Field Performance Approach

The preceding pages have presented a review of the present status of the semi-empirical approach to evaluating the liquefaction resistance of sands and silty sands from measured values of the Standard Penetration Resistance and field performance data. The method may be summarized in a series of steps as follows:

1. For soils at depths shallower than 10 ft., multiply measured N values by 0.75 to allow for energy loss in the drive rods.

2. Convert N values to N_1 values using the C_N correction curves shown in Fig. 47.

3. For sands with $D_{50} > 0.25$ mm use the standard correlation curves for sand shown in Figs. 54 and 57.

4. For silty sands and silts plotting below the A-line and with $D_{50} < 0.15$ mm use

$$N_1 = (N_1)_{measured} + 7.5$$

and then use the standard correlation curves for sands.

5. If the confining pressure exceeds 1.5 tons/sq.ft., reduce the stress ratio causing liquefaction to allow for the reduction due to increased confining pressure. Such reductions may be determined by laboratory tests or on the basis of experience.

6. Consider some clay soils as being vulnerable to significant losses in strength. Based on the Chinese data these soils appear to have the following characteristics:

Percent finer than 0.005 mm < 15%
Liquid Limit (LL) < 35
Water Content > 0.9 LL

The best way to handle these soils, if they plot above the A-line, is to determine their liquefaction characteristics by tests.

7. If the clay content (determined by 0.005 mm) > 20%, consider the soil non-liquefiable, unless it is extremely sensitive.

8. If the water content of any clayey soil (clay, sandy clay, silty clay, clayey sand, etc.) < 0.9 LL, consider the soil non-liquefiable.

It should be noted that in using this approach with the charts presented, the SPT should be determined in the standard method using a rope and pulley system to lift the falling weight, as described previously. If a free-falling weight is used or if there are other deviations from the test procedure used in determining the N_1 values used in the charts shown, judgment must be exercised to evaluate an appropriate N_1 value for the soil before using the charts.

It may also be noted that the chart shown in Fig. 54 is based entirely on field performance of deposits during actual earthquakes and is thus based on a large number of field case studies. Its extension to silty sands is similarly well supported by field case data. Extension of the chart to earthquakes with magnitudes other than $M = 7\frac{1}{2}$ is based on a statistical analysis of many earthquake records and the characteristic shape of a liquefaction curve determined by very large scale cyclic simple shear tests. As such, it is not believed that the use of the scaling factors indicated by this curve will introduce any serious error in the positions of the family of curves shown in Fig. 57.

Because this empirical approach is founded on such a large body of field data, it appears to provide the most useful empirical approach available at the present time. However, it should be noted that the Standard Penetration Test cannot be performed conveniently at all depths (say deeper than 100 ft. or through large depths of water) or in all soils (such as those containing a significant proportion of gravel particles). Thus, it is desirable that it be supplemented by other in-situ test methods which can also be correlated with soil liquefaction potential. In many cases the Static Cone Test, which can be performed more rapidly and more continuously, may provide a good means for evaluating liquefaction potential especially if it is correlated on a site dependent basis with SPT results. However, this procedure also is limited to sands and silty sands. In dealing with soils containing large particles or in difficult environments, other in-situ characteristics such as the shear wave velocity or the electrical characteristics of the soil may provide a more suitable means for assessment of liquefaction potential. In due course, any or all of these in-situ test methods may have their own detailed correlation with field performance to validate their usefulness as meaningful indicators of liquefaction characteristics. It seems likely, however, that for onshore sites with deposits of sand up to 100 ft. deep or so, the correlation of liquefaction characteristics with SPT data will provide the most direct empirical means of evaluating field liquefaction potential for some years to come. Other methods, however, have a significant role to play and should be developed to the fullest extent to provide information for different soil types and environments.

Application of Standard Penetration Test Data
to Evaluate Liquefaction Potential

The applicability of standard penetration test data to evaluate the liquefaction potential of sands can be illustrated by the results of a study, conducted by Clough and Chameau (1981), of the properties of sand fills in the waterfront area of San Francisco and their behavior during the San Francisco earthquake of 1906.

Between 1850 and 1915, over 20 million cu. yds. of fill were placed over the soft Bay Mud along the shoreline of San Francisco to create the waterfront port area, the depth of fill ranging up to 40 ft. In the early stages, fill was placed mainly in an area called Yerba Buena Cove and a considerable quantity of fill consisted of dune sands which were plentifully available on the eastern side of San Francisco. The sands and other materials were generally dumped into place with no compaction.

During the 1906 San Francisco earthquake (Magnitude $\approx$ 8.3) heavy damage attributed to liquefaction developed in three of the fill areas although other areas showed no apparent effects of liquefaction. In their study, Clough and Chameau made detailed soil explorations at two sites, one where liquefaction was known to have occurred in the old Yerba Buena Cove area (the YBC site) and one near Telegraph Hill showing no evidence of liquefaction (the TH site). In both areas the soil profile consisted of about 10 ft. of rubble fill, 20 to 30 ft. of sand and 20 to 30 ft. of soft clay underlain by stiffer soils to a total depth of about 80 ft. The water table was about 5 ft. below the ground surface.

It may be noted that during the 1906 earthquake the soft Bay Mud was apparently stable since buildings supported on piles embedded in the Bay Mud had generally excellent performance. Thus the liquefaction in the YBC area was apparently limited to the sand deposit extending to about 30 ft. below the ground surface.

Standard penetration tests made at the two sites showed considerable scatter in penetration resistance values but average values were as follows:

Depth	Average SPT value		Normalized N-value, N_1	
	TH site	YBC site	TH site	YBC site
10 ft.	15	13	23	20
15 ft.	21	13	26	16
20 ft.	25	13	29	15
25 ft.	30	13	33	14
30 ft.	34	13	34	13

Clough and Chameau used ground response analyses to determine the maximum ground surface accelerations. The sites are both located about 10 miles from the causative fault of the 1906 earthquake and could be expected to have a peak acceleration in rock of about 0.5g. Based on this rock acceleration, the maximum ground acceleration was computed to be about 0.31g. It may be noted that the maximum ground surface acceleration for sites underlain by soft to medium stiff clays as read off from Fig. 19 would be about 0.28g.

For a ground surface acceleration of 0.30g, the cyclic stress ratio induced in the sand at a depth of 15 ft. may be computed as follows:

$$\sigma_o \approx 15 \times 110 = 1650 \, psf$$

$$\sigma_o' \approx 5 \times 110 + 10 \times 55 = 1100 \, psf$$

$$\frac{\tau_{av}}{\sigma_o'} \approx 0.65 \cdot \frac{a_{max}}{g} \cdot \frac{\sigma_o}{\sigma_o'} \cdot r_d$$

$$\approx 0.65 \cdot 0.30 \cdot \frac{1650}{1100} \cdot 0.95$$

$$\approx 0.27$$

At a depth of 25 ft. the stress ratio developed, computed by a similar procedure, is 0.31.

Thus the induced stress ratios and corresponding N_1 values for the two sites are as follows:

Depth	Induced Stress Ratio	N_1 values		Stress Ratio for Liquefaction (from Fig. 57)	
		TH site	YBC site	TH site	YBC site
15 ft.	0.27	26	16	0.26	0.16
25 ft.	0.31	33	14	0.35	0.14

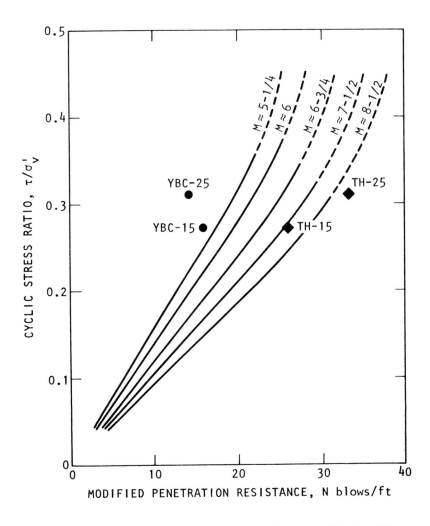

Figure 60. Chart for evaluation of liquefaction potential for different magnitude earthquakes.

Comparison of the induced stress ratios with the stress ratios causing liquefaction shows that the Telegraph Hill site is marginally stable and the Yerba Buena Cove site is clearly unstable. The induced stress ratios and N_1 values can be plotted on the chart for evaluating liquefaction potential as shown in Fig. 60. It may be seen that the field data for the Yerba Buena Cove site shows this area to be clearly vulnerable to liquefaction in a Magnitude 8 earthquake but the data for the Telegraph Hill site shows this area to be marginally safe. The predicted performance is thus quite similar to the observed performance at both test sites.

Factor of Safety in Evaluating Liquefaction or Cyclic Mobility Potential

In evaluating the liquefaction or cyclic mobility potential of a saturated sand deposit under some postulated earthquake condition, it is customary to express the results in terms of a factor of safety against liquefaction or unacceptable performance as:

$$\text{Factor of Safety} = \frac{\tau_\ell}{\tau_d}$$

where τ_ℓ = Average cyclic stress required to cause liquefaction or cyclic mobility in N cycles

and τ_d = Average cyclic stress induced by earthquake for N cycles

This requires determinations of the stresses induced by the earthquake and the stresses which must be applied to the sand to cause liquefaction or a given level of cyclic mobility (defined as the development of an unacceptable level of strain) if this is more appropriate.

If the earthquake motions are specified at the ground surface, then the stresses developed in the upper 40 ft. of soil can readily be assessed by simplified procedures. For greater depths, simplified procedures become increasingly less accurate and ground response analysis may be required. Whichever method is used, some uncertainties may well occur except for shallow depths.

Uncertainties will also exist in the determination of the stresses required to cause liquefaction or a given level of strain. The final acceptable factor of safety will depend on the accuracy with which each of these individual determinations can be made in any given case and on the conservatism introduced in other aspects of the evaluation.

As a general guideline, acceptable factors of safety range from about 1.25 to 1.5, though values outside this range may sometimes be accepted. A careful assessment of the consequences of overestimating the factor of safety should be made, however, when factors of safety less than about 1.4 are allowed. Similarly, in dealing with dense sands, consideration should be given to the possibly minor consequences of underestimating the factor of safety.

CONCLUSIONS

In the preceding pages an attempt has been made to summarize, in as simple a way as possible, the essential elements of the current state of the art for evaluating the liquefaction or cyclic mobility potential of soil deposits on level ground due to earthquake shaking. Clearly there is still much to learn but it appears that progress in understanding and evaluating soil liquefaction during the past 15 years has led to a state of knowledge where engineers can now evaluate these phenomena with an adequate degree of reliability for design purposes.

It would seem that the design engineer confronted with the need to evaluate the liquefaction or cyclic mobility potential of a deposit has two basic choices if he considers it appropriate to neglect the possible effects of drainage occurring during the period of cyclic stress application:

1. To calculate the stresses induced in the ground by the design earthquake, using either ground response analyses or simplified procedures, whichever seems most appropriate, and to compare these stresses with those required to cause liquefaction or cyclic mobility of representative samples in the laboratory. The main problem in this approach will lie in

correctly assessing the characteristics of the in-situ deposit from laboratory tests performed on even good quality undisturbed samples. Because of the potential variations in the effect of sample disturbance on the measured characteristics of undisturbed samples, considerable judgment will be required in this endeavor. There is evidence to indicate that this may not be a serious problem for medium dense sands with relative densities of the order of 50 percent but it is likely to be a dominant effect for dense and very dense sands. Or

2. To be guided by the known field performance of sand deposits correlated with some measure of in-situ characteristics, such as the standard penetration test, on the grounds that most factors which tend to improve cyclic mobility or liquefaction resistance also tend to increase the standard penetration resistance or the results of any other in-situ test which may be adopted as a possible indicator of field liquefaction behavior. Thus the stress ratios likely to cause liquefaction or significant shear strains may be read from a design chart such as that shown in Fig. 57. Judgment may well be necessary to evaluate the applicability of standard penetration test data if conventional procedures are not used.

It is apparent that judgment is required whichever method is used. In the best situations it should be possible to obtain reasonable agreement on the potential for liquefaction or cyclic mobility using both of the available approaches. However, since it would be imprudent ever to neglect the guidance to be derived from records of past experience, the results obtained by this approach should always be used as a primary guide unless there is good reason to doubt their applicability in any given case.

References

1. Applied Technology Council, *Tentative Provisions for the Development of Seismic Regulations for Buildings,* Pub. No. ATC-3-06, Applied Technology Council, Palo Alto, CA, 1978.

2. Bieganousky, W. A. and W. F. Marcuson, III, *Liquefaction of Dams and Foundations—Report 1: Laboratory Standard Penetration Test on Reid Bedford Model and Ottawa Sands,* WES Report S-76-2, Oct 1976.

3. Campbell, K. W., "Near-Source Attenuation of Peak Horizontal Acceleration," *Bull. Seis. Soc. Amer.,* 71:6, Dec 1981, pp. 2039-2070.

4. Castro, G., "Liquefaction and Cyclic Mobility of Saturated Sands," *Jnl. Geotechnical Eng. Div., ASCE,* 101:GT6, Jun 1975, pp. 551-569.

5. Cloud, W. K., "Intensity Map and Structural Damage, Parkfield, California, Earthquake of June 27, 1966," *Bull. Seis. Soc. Amer.,* 57:6, Dec 1967, pp. 1161-1179.

6. Clough, G. W. and J.-L. Chameau, *Seismic Response of San Francisco Waterfront Fills,* ASCE Preprint 81-544, ASCE National Convention, St. Louis, Oct 1981.

7. DeAlba, P., H. B. Seed, and C. K. Chan, "Sand Liquefaction in Large-Scale Simple Shear Tests," *Jnl. Geotechnical Eng. Div., ASCE,* 102:GT9, Proc. Paper 12403, Sep 1976, pp. 909-927.

8. Douglas, B. J., R. S. Olsen, and G. R. Martin, "Evaluation of Cone Penetrometer Test for SPT Liquefaction Assessment," in *Insitu Testing to Evaluate Liquefaction Susceptibility,* ASCE Preprint 81-544, ASCE National Convention, St. Louis, Oct 1981.

9. "Earthquake-Resistant Design Code for Industrial and Civil Buildings," TJ11-74, State Capital Construction Commission, China Building Publishing House, Peking, China, Dec 1974, (trans. by Andrew C. S. Chang).

10. Finn, W. D. L., K. W. Lee, and G. R. Martin, "An Effective Stress Model for Liquefaction," *Jnl. Geotechnical Eng. Div., ASCE,* 103:GT6, Jun 1977, pp. 517–533.

11. Gibbs, H. J. and W. G. Holtz, "Research on Determining the Density of Sands by Spoon Penetrating Testing," *Proc. Fourth Inter. Conf. on Soil Mechanics and Foundation Engineering,* London, 1957.

12. Housner, G. W., "Spectrum Intensities of Strong-Motion Earthquakes," *Proc. Symp. on Earthquake and Blast Effects on Structures,* Earthquake Engineering Research Institute, Berkeley, CA, Jun 1952, pp. 20–36.

13. Housner, G. W., "Behavior of Structures During Earthquakes," *Jnl. Eng. Mech. Div., ASCE,* 85:EM4, Oct 1959, pp. 109–129.

14. Hudson, D. E., "Response Spectrum Techniques in Engineering Seismology," *Proc. First World Conf. on Earthquake Engineering,* Berkeley, CA, 1956.

15. Hudson, D. E., *Reading and Interpreting Strong Motion Accelerograms,* Earthquake Engineering Research Institute, Berkeley, CA, 1979.

16. Idriss, I. M., "Characteristics of Earthquake Ground Motions," *Proc. ASCE Geotechnical Eng. Div. Specialty Conf. on Earthquake Engineering and Soil Dynamics,* Vol. III, Pasadena, CA, Jun 1978, pp. 1151–1265.

17. Idriss, I. M., I. Arango, and G. Brogan, *Study of Liquefaction in November 23, 1977 Earthquake, San Juan Province, Argentina,* Woodward-Clyde Consultants, San Francisco, Oct 1979.

18. Idriss, I. M. and H. B. Seed, "An Analysis of Ground Motions During the 1957 San Francisco Earthquake," *Bull. Seis. Soc. Amer.,* 58:6, Dec 1968, pp. 2013–2032.

19. Ishihara, K. "Pore Water Pressure Rises during Earthquakes," *Proc. Inter. Conf. on Recent Advances in Geotechnical Earthquake Engineering and Soil Dynamics,* St. Louis, Vol. 3, May 1981, pp. 1–4.

20. Ishihara, K. and Y. Koga, "Case Studies of Liquefaction in the 1964 Niigata Earthquake," Soils and Foundations, Japanese Soc. of Soil Mechanics and Foundation Engineering, 21:3, Sep 1981, pp. 35–52.

21. Joyner, W. B. and D. M. Boore, "Peak Horizontal Acceleration and Velocity from Strong-Motion Records Including Records from the 1979 Imperial Valley, California, Earthquake," *Bull. Seis. Soc. Amer.* 71:6, Dec 1981, pp. 2011–2038.

22. Kishida, H., "Damage to Reinforced Concrete Buildings in Niigata City with Special Reference to Foundation Engineering," Soils and Foundations, Japanese Soc. of Soil Mechanics and Foundation Engineering, 7:1, 1966.

23. Koizumi, Y., "Changes in Density of Sand Subsoil Caused by the Niigata Earthquake," Soils and Foundations, Japanese Soc. of Soil Mechanics and Foundation Engineering, 6:2, Mar 1966, pp. 38–44.

24. Kovacs, W. D., *Velocity Measurement of a Free-Fall Hammer,* 1978.

25. Kovacs, W. D., J. C. Evans, and A. H. Griffith, "Towards a More Standardized SPT," *Proc. Ninth Inter. Conf. on Soil Mechanics and Foundation Engineering,* Tokyo, 1977.

26. Lee, K. L. and A. Albeisa, "Earthquake Induced Settlements in Saturated Sands," *Jnl. Soil Mechanics and Foundations Div. ASCE,* 100:GT4, Apr 1974, pp. 387–406.

27. Liou, C. P., V. L. Streeter, and F. E. Richart, "A Numerical Model for Liquefaction," *Jnl. Geotechnical Eng. Div., ASCE,* 103:GT6, Jun 1977, pp. 589–606.

28. LNG Seismic Review Panel (L. S. Cluff, Chairman), *Seismic Safety Review of the Proposed Liquefied Natural Gas Facility, Little Cojo Bay, Santa Barbara County, California,* Report to California Public Utilities Commission, Nov 1981.

29. MacMurdo, J., "Papers Relating to the Earthquake which Occurred in India in 1819," *Phil. Mag.,* Vol. 63, 1824, pp. 105–

177. (Also in *Royal Asiatic Society of London and Dublin,* Bombay Branch, Vol. 3, pp. 90–116, 1823.)

30. Marcuson, W. F., III and W. A. Bieganousky, "Laboratory Standard Penetration Tests on Fine Sands," *Jnl. Geotechnical Eng. Div., ASCE,* 103:GT6, Jun 1977, pp. 565–588.

31. Marcuson, W. F., III and G. Franklin, *Undisturbed Sampling of Cohesionless Soils,* State-of-the-Art Report, Singapore, 1979.

32. Martin, G. R., W. D. L. Finn, and H. B. Seed, "Fundamentals of Liquefaction under Cyclic Loading," *Jnl. Geotechnical Eng. Div., ASCE,* 101:GT5, May 1975, pp. 423–438.

33. Martin, P. P. and H. B. Seed, "Simplified Procedure for Effective Stress Analysis of Ground Response," *Jnl. Geotechnical Eng. Div., ASCE,* 105:GT6, Jun 1979, pp. 739–758.

34. Merino y Coronado, J., "El Tremblor del 28 de Julio de 1957," *Anales Inst. de Geofis,* University of Mexico, 3, 1957.

35. Newmark, N. M., Consulting Engineering Services, *A Study of Vertical and Horizontal Earthquake Spectra,* Directorate of Licensing, U. S. Atomic Energy Commission, Washington D.C., 1973.

36. Nuttli, O. W. and R. B. Herrmann, *Consequences of Earthquakes in the Mississippi Valley,* ASCE Preprint 81–519, ASCE National Convention, St. Louis, Oct 1981.

37. Ohsaki, Y., "Niigata Earthquakes, 1964 Building Damage and Condition," Soils and Foundations, Japanese Soc. of Soil Mechanics and Foundation Engineering, 6:2, Mar 1966, pp. 14–37.

38. Palacios, A., *The Theory and Measurement of Energy Transfer During SPT Test Sampling,* Ph.D. dissertation, Univ. of Florida, 1977.

39. Porcella, R. L. and R. B. Matthiesen, USGS Open-File Report 79–1654, 1979.

40. Rosenblueth, E., "The Earthquake of 28 July 1957 in Mexico City," *Proc. Second World Conf. on Earthquake Engineering,* Japan, Vol. I, 1960.

41. Ross, G. A., H. B. Seed, and R. R. Migliaccio, "Bridge Foundation Behavior in Alaska Earthquake," *Jnl. Soil Mechanics and Foundations Div., ASCE,* 94:SM4, Jul 1969, pp. 1007-1036.

42. Sadigh, K. et al., Personal communication, 1979.

43. Schmertmann, J. H., *Predicting the q_c/N Ratio—Interpreting the Dynamics of the Standard Penetration Test,* Univ. of Florida Report to the Dept. of Transportation, Florida, Oct 1976.

44. Schmertmann, J. H., "Use the SPT to Measure Dynamic Properties?—Yes, But . . . !" *Proc. American Society for Testing and Materials Symposium on Dynamic Field and Laboratory Testing of Soil and Rock,* Denver, Jun 1977.

45. Schmertmann, J. H., *Guidelines for Cone Penetration Test Performance and Design,* FHWA–TS–78–209, U.S. Dept. of Transportation, Federal Highway Admin., Washington D.C., Jul 1978.

46. Seed, H. B., "Soil Problems and Soil Behavior," Chapter 10 of *Earthquake Engineering,* R. L. Wiegel, Coord. Ed. Prentice-Hall, Englewood Cliffs, N.J., 1970, pp. 227-251.

47. Seed, H. B., "Landslides During Earthquakes Due to Liquefaction," *Jnl. Soil Mechanics and Foundations Div., ASCE,* 94:SM5, Sep 1968, pp. 1053-1122.

48. Seed, H. B., "Soil Liquefaction and Cyclic Mobility Evaluation for Level Ground during Earthquakes," *Jnl. Geotechnical Eng. Div., ASCE,* 105:GT2, Feb 1979, pp. 201-255.

49. Seed, H. B. and G. Alonso, Jose Luis "Effects of Soil-Structure Interaction in the Caracas Earthquake of 1967," *Proc. First Venezuelan Conf. on Seismology and Earthquake Engineering,* Oct 1974.

50. Seed, H. B., I. Arango, C. K. Chan, A. Gomez-Masso, and R. G. Ascoli, "Earthquake-Induced Liquefaction Near Lake Amatitlan, Guatemala," *Jnl. Geotechnical Eng. Div., ASCE,* 107:GT4, Apr 1981, pp. 501-518.

51. Seed, H. B. and I. M. Idriss, "Analysis of Soil Liquefaction:

Niigata Earthquake," *Jnl. Soil Mechanics and Foundations Div., ASCE,* 93:SM3, May 1967, pp. 83–108.

52. Seed, H. B. and I. M. Idriss, "Simplified Procedure for Evaluating Soil Liquefaction Potential," *Jnl. Soil Mechanics and Foundations Div., ASCE,* 97:SM9, Sep 1971, pp. 1249–1273.

53. Seed, H. B. and I. M. Idriss, "Evaluation of Liquefaction Potential using Field Performance Data," Accepted for pub. in *Jnl. Geotechnical Eng. Div., ASCE,* 1982.

54. Seed, H. B., I. M. Idriss, F. Makdisi, and N. Banerjee, *Representation of Irregular Stress Time Histories by Equivalent Uniform Stress Series in Liquefaction Analyses,* EERC 75-29, Earthquake Engineering Research Center, Univ. of California, Berkeley, Oct 1975.

55. Seed, H. B., K. L. Lee, I. M. Idriss, and F. I. Makdisi, "The Slides in the San Fernando Dams During the Earthquake of February 9, 1971," *Jnl. Geotechnical Eng. Div., ASCE,* 101:GT7, Jul 1975, pp. 651–688.

56. Seed, H. B., P. P. Martin, and J. Lysmer, "Pore-Water Pressure Changes during Soil Liquefaction," *Jnl. Geotechnical Eng. Div., ASCE,* 102:GT4, Apr 1976, pp. 323–346.

57. Seed, H. B., K. Mari, and C. K. Chan, *Influence of Seismic History on the Liquefaction Characteristics of Sands,* EERC 75-25, Earthquake Engineering Research Center, Univ. of California, Berkeley, Aug 1975.

58. Seed, H. B. and W. H. Peacock, "Test Procedures for Measuring Soil Liquefaction Characteristics," *Jnl. Soil Mechanics and Foundations Div., ASCE,* 97:SM8, Aug 1971, pp. 1099–1119.

59. Seed, H. B., R. Pyke, and G. R. Martin, *Analysis of the Effect of Multi-directional Shaking on the Liquefaction Characteristics of Sands,* EERC 75-41, Earthquake Engineering Research Center, Univ. of California, Berkeley, Dec 1975.

60. Seed, H. B., S. Singh, C. K. Chan, and T. F. Vilela, "Considerations in Undisturbed Sampling of Sands," *Jnl. Geotechnical Eng. Div., ASCE,* 108:GT2, Feb 1982, pp. 265–283.

61. Seed, H. B., C. Ugas, and J. Lysmer, "Site-Dependent Spectra for Earthquake-Resistant Design," *Bull. Seis. Soc. Amer.,* 66:1, Feb 1976, pp. 221–243.

62. Seed, H. B. and S. D. Wilson, "The Turnagain Heights Landslide, Anchorage, Alaska," *Jnl. Soil Mechanics and Foundations Div., ASCE,* 93:SM4, Jul 1967, pp. 325–353.

63. Tatsuoka, F., T. Iwasaki, K. Tokida, S. Yasuda, M. Hirose, T. Imai, and M. Kon-no, "Standard Penetration Tests and Soil Liquefaction Potential Evaluation," Soils and Foundations, Japanese Soc. of Soil Mechanics and Foundation Engineering, 20:4, Dec 1980.

64. Tokimatsu, K. and Y. Yoshimi, "Field Correlation of Soil Liquefaction with SPT and Grain Size," *Proc. Inter. Conf. on Recent Advances in Geotechnical Earthquake Engineering and Soil Dynamics,* St. Louis, Apr–May 1981.

65. Trifunac, M. D. and A. G. Brady, "Correlation of Peak Acceleration, Velocity and Displacement with Earthquake Magnitude, Distance and Site Conditions," *Earthquake Engineering and Structural Dynamics Jnl.,* 4:5, 1976.

66. Wahler Associates Geotechnical Engineers, *Seismic Reevaluation of Camanche Reservoir Main Dam,* Project EBM-106A for East Bay Municipal Utility District, Jan 1981.

67. Wang, W., "Some Findings in Soil Liquefaction," Water Conservancy and Hydroelectric Power Scientific Research Institute, Beijing, China, Aug 1979.

68. Wood, H. O., "Distribution of Apparent Intensity in San Francisco," in *The California Earthquake of April 18, 1906,* Report of the State Earthquake Investigation Commission, Carnegie Institution of Washington, Washington D.C., pp. 220–245.

69. Xie, J., "Empirical Criteria for Sand Liquefaction," *Proc. Second U. S. National Conf. on Earthquake Engineering,* Stanford Univ., Aug 1979.

70. Youd, T. L. and S. N. Hoose, "Liquefaction Susceptibility and

Geologic Setting," *Proc. Sixth World Conf. on Earthquake Engineering,* New Delhi, Vol. III, pp. 2189–2194.

71. Zhou, S. G., "Influence of Fines on Evaluating Liquefaction of Sand by SPT," *Proc. Inter. Conf. on Recent Advances in Geotechnical Earthquake Engineering and Soil Dynamics,* St. Louis, Vol. 2, May 1981, pp. 167–172.